How To Start A YouTube Channel

The Easy Way

with

Charlie & Friends

Written & Illustrated by Emma Drew

Acknowledgements

Thank you to my dear children who have inspired, encouraged and helped me to write and illustrate this book. Thank you to Claire Jennison who's editing magic and positive energy kept me going to the end.

Thanks to YouTube creators Lucy Wyndham-Read (Lucy Wyndham-Read), Dan Bull (Dan Bull), Maggy Woodley (Red Ted Art), Luke Ayios (MiffedCrew), Connor Colquhoun (CDawgVA), Oli Greaves (OGXtailor), Aaron Abke (Aaron Abke), Ieva & Sunshine (Surprise Collector & Sunshine), Greg Holgate (The Stupendium), Sam (Sam The Kid Gaming) and Emma (MyVoxSongs) who contributed their valuable YouTube wisdom and advice.

Thank you to YouTube, TubeBuddy, Wikipedia, Canva, Gimp and Amazon for making it possible to become an independent creator.

The information in this book is for educational purposes. British spellings are used throughout this book.

Chapter 8 offers a list of useful and informative online safety kids' support groups, resources & articles for kids, parents, guardians and teachers. The intended purpose is to bring awareness to these charities and organisations that tirelessly support families and are helping make a difference to online safeguarding.

All the resources listed on these pages are for information only. While every effort has been made to ensure accuracy, the author cannot accept responsibility for the content or changes made by these websites, apps, organisations or their services. Some Chapter 8 pages with clickable links can be found at OnlineMediaBiz.com/Books. If you are a relevant charity or organisation and want to be included in the list, please contact the author.

This book has been independently created based on the author's own experience as a professional YouTube creator. It has not been written in partnership or affiliation with Google or YouTube or any other company. The author may gain a small commission on corresponding affiliate links associated with products or services recommended in this book. This will be denoted by AFF in corresponding site links.

Written, illustrated and fonts by Emma Drew

Published by Online Media Biz Publishing

ISBN: 978-1-8384406-6-4

Edition 2

With love to my beautiful kids

…and the home kitties, Kiki and Totoro

Hello Video Creators! This is your ultimate YouTube companion.

This book will help you learn how to easily make fabulous YouTube videos, and have fun doing it.

Table of Contents

Chapter 1

INTRODUCTION

CHAPTER 1: INTRODUCTION

Hello friend, welcome to my little space on YouTube. I'm one of the original YouTube creator cats, **Charlie**, the curious one. A little birdie told me that you wanted to be a YouTube creator too, so I'm here to help. It's important to start your YouTube channel in the right way, but I'm going to show you how to do it the **easy** way!

A BIT ABOUT ME

So, who am I exactly and why should you listen to me? I'm Charlie. Check out my profile below for more facts about me.

Us cats got some flack for taking over the internet when you were a young kid, or possibly before you were even born. Remember those days when it took more than 10 seconds to buffer a video? Ah, maybe you don't, but I bet your parents do! Luckily, we don't see much of that anymore, although there are one or two other technical hitches we still face: **"You have low battery!"** and **"Your device has no storage!"** to name just a few.

Thankfully, we've moved on from back then in leaps and bounds. Now, you can make and upload videos **whenever** you want on almost **anything** you like, pretty much **instantaneously**.

I've been doing this YouTube thing for over 10 years. I've filmed this, animated that, game-played the other, designed the merch and bought the T-shirt (my own of course!). Now it's time to show you how I did it and how **YOU** can do it too....by the end of this book you shall be a YouTube aficionado, guaranteed!

When I was just a cute kitten, I wanted to share my videos with the whole world. I went to every publishing house, every TV company, every animation studio and **nothing**. No luck. **NADA, NADA, NADA!** (BTW 'nada' means 'nothing' in Spanish.) Nobody was interested in sharing my videos on their TV channels. Needless to say, I was quite disappointed. Poor me. ☹

I never let that stop me though. My curiosity was too strong, my creativity kept pouring out, and even though Art was my favourite subject at school, I just wanted to make **videos**.

One day I sat down with my drawing pad, my computer, music, snacks and – most importantly – my **imagination!** I spent a few days enjoying my ideas, doodling, creating and drawing characters. I started to put these together in a mini flipbook to make a little animation, and then I transferred it onto a drawing app.

Then, I heard about a little website called **YouTube**, where anyone could add videos with the aim of **entertaining everyone**. This website was the awesome idea of three dudes called **Steve** Chen, **Chad** Hurley and **Jawed** Karim.

The most interesting bit about this website was that, apparently, the creators came up with the idea while living above a **pizza** shop!

That must have been rather convenient for them, don't you think? I've heard pizza is a super food and clearly it proved to provide great inspiration for inventing **YouTube**. I don't know about you but it's definitely my secret ingredient whenever I need a bit of **super creative video inspiration**! I'll be talking more about special ingredients a little later on.

TIPS AND TRICKS:

- Never touch the camera lens with greasy pizza fingers.
- Eat your pizza before or after recording but never while filming! (Unless you're recording a video about how to make a pizza). It can get a little messy.
- Guard this book against younger (and older!) siblings (and pets) and other family members.
- Read it to the end and keep it as your ultimate video companion to experience some very creative video making magic!

At the time I had no idea that this one little website called YouTube would allow me to conquer the internet – as a fictional character, you understand. No need for any talent agencies or TV judge culture.

This was so exciting for me and totally 'pawsome' (I know, I know, I really must stop these paw cat jokes. I'll try my best for you human folk). I set to work. I created characters, animated videos and uploaded them to YouTube. Ten years later I became a **very satisfied YouTube cat creator pro** with lots of views and subscribers, which showed my work was being enjoyed and attracting fans. I kept going because I loved making videos so much and I am now a proud owner of my very own **YouTube Play Button**. It took a few years, but hey, who's counting?

Glossary: YouTube Play Buttons form part of the YouTube Creator Awards. They are a series of gifts from YouTube that aim to recognise those channels that have climbed to the top of the charts. Each channel is reviewed to make sure that it follows the YouTube community guidelines before an award is given out.

I have been fortunate enough to have entertained millions of people all over the world with my animation videos. So, what's my secret? How did I do it?

The **SECRET** is that there is **no secret!** Just lots of **tips, tricks** and – most importantly – lots of **practice**. In order to help you through your video making journey, I've asked my **BFFs** to join me in guiding you lovely peeps with their **YouTube tips**, help and specialist knowledge.

MEET MY YOUTUBE FRIENDS

Charlie

Hey guys, I'm happy you could all join me in this book. Please introduce yourselves to these budding video makers.

Marvela

Encantado! I'm **Marvela**. I can help you plan your video ideas. (BTW 'encantado' means 'pleased to meet you' in Spanish.)

Cherrybelle

Hiya, I'm **Cherrybelle**. I love making all types of video.

Prof. Alga Rhythm

Hello. I'm **Professor Alga Rhythm** but you can call me **Alga.** I love coding and music.

Sam

Hey dudes and dudettes, I'm Sammy but you can call me **Sam**. I'm a whizz in the YouTube creator studio.

Ted

Hi, I'm **Ted**. Wassup? My favourite bit about making video is the editing.

So, **how do you begin making YouTube videos** the easy way?

Before we start, let's be sure we know the ground rules and talk about the **official YouTube account guidelines**. Read them before starting your channel and stay safe with online video!

STAY SAFE ONLINE: THE RULES

In most countries YouTube is for people aged 13 years old and over. If you're under 13 years old you will have to wait until you're older however you can still make your own videos. The good thing is you can spend your spare time learning, experimenting and practising making awesome videos, even if you can't upload them to YouTube.

If you are aged 13 to 17 (depending on your country) you can set up a YouTube channel account, but you **MUST get permission from a parent or guardian**. Your parent(s) or guardian(s) can help you by supervising your video uploads, comments and channel interactions, including your channel settings (they're always super helpful for this bit so get them involved). This means that **when you're 16/17+ you are likely to be a well-trained YouTube video making pro**.

YouTube channels made for kids have a lot of features disabled, such as the comments and community tabs. They are turned off to help **keep you safe** from potentially undesirable content and to create a **safe place** where you can focus on creating your awesome videos.

See the backstage area (Chapter 8) for more ways to stay safe online and see how you can help make the internet safer for you and your friends and family.

PRIVACY

I recommend setting all your YouTube video uploads to **private**. Make sure a parent or guardian watches and approves your videos before you press **publish** and unleash them onto the digital world.

Glossary: Publish. A YouTube video can be uploaded but is only seen by viewers when it is made live or published. YouTube has three settings for each video: published, private and unlisted.

EXPRESS TO IMPRESS

As your companion, this book aims to give you a great start in **video making** so you can have some real fun and **easily express your creative ideas**. You will be able to:

- Impress your friends and family with your **advanced video knowledge** and abilities! Don't forget to **impress yourself** while you're at it! Be proud of your video creations.
- Learn the latest super cool video tech skills that will **bedazzle** your viewers!
- Become a **multi talented film or documentary maker** that tells amazing stories using video!

- Unleash your creative spirit onto an unsuspecting world and create a **community of fantastic fans**! **FANS-TASTIC**!
- Eat super foods like **PIZZA** while making your videos!

YOUTUBE FACTS AND STATS

DID YOU KNOW…

If you're like me and want to know a few facts and stats about YouTube then read on. They can be particularly handy for those family quiz get-togethers! If you're not interested in this stuff just skip to the next section.

FACT ALERT #1:

YouTube is the biggest video website in the world. The most surprising fact of all is that the videos are not all cat videos. Shocking I know…

FACT ALERT #2:

YouTube is watched by almost a **third of the world's population!** That's like 2 billion peeps or more. No wonder they keep going on about **staying safe online.**

FACT ALERT #3:

Over **500 hours of video** are uploaded to YouTube every minute. That's almost 50 hours of videos uploaded every **SECOND.**

WOWZERS. That's a lot of facts and stats but take it from me…the biggest **FACT** is: making videos is **EASY and SO MUCH FUN!**

So, let's get started…

Firstly, YouTube is a video website where you can **share your ideas** with people interested in your video topics. Contrary to popular belief it is NOT all about **Lamborghinis**, **video games** and **pranks**. There's a lot of **hard work**, **passion** and **dedication** that goes into being a **YouTube pro**.

So, let's get this straight.

YouTube is NOT:

A race to the top of the views and subscriber lists.

A competition to have the best video or channel in the world.

A popularity contest.

A **YouTube** channel is a bit like having a **website** or blog but instead of lots of text and writing it is made up of videos. You can showcase your special talent or message with videos on your channel and create a place where your community of fans can appreciate your work and enjoy being part of the same group. It's a bit like a club.

HOW TO BE A YOUTUBER

In my cat eyes, you are technically a **YouTube creator** as soon as you come up with a few ideas for your YouTube channel and start turning those ideas into videos!

There are **TWO things every YouTube creator pro has in common with you**:

1. They were a **kid** once, just like you.
2. They started their YouTube channel with **zero views and subscribers**.

I love seeing the early videos of my favourite YouTubers. All your favourite **YouTubers had to start somewhere**. As they continued making and uploading videos, they had to think of lots of ways they could improve their content and editing skills in order to **grow** into the YouTube creator they are today.

If you're a curious cat like me, you can easily **check out your favourite YouTubers' early videos** too. You can see what topics they started with and the way they edited their videos at the beginning of their journey, then compare how they have changed topics or developed their style over time.

You can also check out their early **hairstyles**! BTW, more often than not their early videos can be a little less slick and polished (and in my case a little embarrassing, but the less said about that the better!).

Checking out their early videos is a fantastic way to see how your favourite YouTubers have **developed**, and you'll see that their first few videos were probably not as fine-tuned as they are today...

TIPS AND TRICKS:

If you want to see your favourite YouTubers' first few videos, this is how to do it:

- Pick your favourite YouTubers' channels
- Go to their channel homepage
- Select the 'videos' tab in the menu bar
- Select the 'filter' drop down
- Select 'earliest videos'

How are they different from their recent video uploads and how have they changed?

...check MEOWT and ENJOY the show.

Glossary: YouTube channel homepage. This is the main YouTube channel webpage. It contains the channel menu, channel artwork, description about videos, a trailer video and all uploaded videos. YouTube creators can customise their homepage.

Q&A

Marvela

What's a YouTube creator?

Charlie

A YouTube creator is someone who makes videos and shares their videos on the YouTube website.

Cherrybelle

So, what's a YouTube influencer?

Charlie

A YouTube influencer is someone who has a YouTube channel that has developed a community of fans within a certain genre or on a specific topic. Some influencers have hundreds, thousands or even millions of subscribers and views. However, you don't need a large number of subscribers and views to be a YouTube creator. You just need a few people who enjoy watching your videos.

Q&A

Ted

How long does it take to become a YouTube creator?

Charlie

It depends on how much time you put into making and uploading videos to YouTube. Most **YouTube creators** can take about a year to grow their channel. Some take less time and some take a lot longer.

Just remember, no two creators are the same. It's your **space** so always go at your own **pace** as it's not a **race**! **Oooh** there's some fancy rhyming there, it's almost a **rap**! Anyway, do what feels comfortable and enjoyable for you.

Chapter 2

SET-UP

CHAPTER 2: SET UP

WHY DO YOU WANT A YOUTUBE CHANNEL?

It's always important to know **WHY** you want to make YouTube videos. How would making videos and having a YouTube channel make you feel? How would it help in achieving your goals? Knowing this helps you stay focussed and keeps you on track.

So, let's dive in a bit deeper. **WHY do you want to make videos** when you could do something less complicated instead, like watching other people's videos, playing video games, or making pizza in real life? You might not always know the answer but it's important to **ask the question** as it helps you discover your interests better.

For example, I have a close friend who wanted a channel because she loved drawing and making frame by frame hand drawn animation. She wanted to share her work with other people who enjoyed watching simple 2D animation.

WHY do you want to start a YouTube channel? To help you answer this question check out the list of reasons below. Do any apply to you?

Reasons for starting a YouTube channel

I want to start a **YouTube channel** because I want to...(tick the main reasons from the list below that you feel best apply to you)

I want to become a YouTuber because I want to...
(tick all the reasons that apply to you)

- [ ] have fun
- [ ] be a full-time YouTuber pro when I'm older
- [ ] have fans and followers
- [ ] teach people what I know / can do

- [ ] share my gaming videos
- [ ] be an influencer

- [ ] share my music
- [ ] entertain people with my talent, comedy, music, art
- [ ] create pranks or challenges
- [ ] share my opinion and review stuff

- [ ] sell merch
- [ ] help change the world to be a better place
- [ ] give me something to do and be less bored
- [ ] be rich
- [ ] become the biggest YouTuber ever
- [ ] make YouTube & Netflix series originals and movies
- [ ] be a cool filmmaker
- [ ] talk about history

- [ ] talk about my POV
- [ ] learn how media works
- [ ] be famous
- [ ] other (write your reasons below)

____

____

____

Have you figured out **WHY** you want to have a great YouTube channel?

It's normal to not be sure when you're starting out. If you already know, **FANTASTIC**. If you don't know, come back to this section at a later date and try again. Sometimes it takes a while to know. You will figure it out **eventually!**

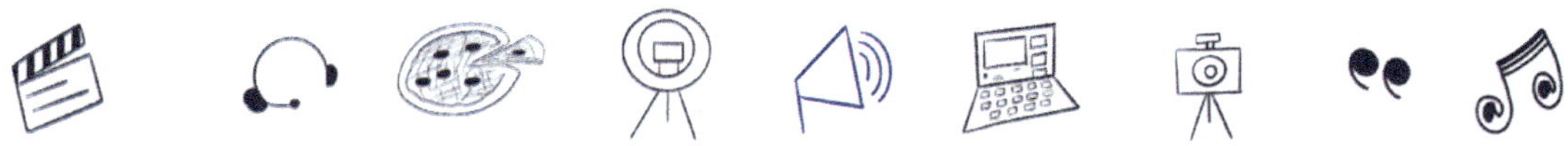

WHAT YOU NEED TO BE AN AWESOME YOUTUBER

As I'm here to help you **become a fabulous YouTube creator**, this section outlines what you will need. Here's a simple list:

1. **You** – the YouTube creator. **You're the most important thing!**
2. Great **ideas** or **topics** for your videos
3. **Camera** recording equipment of some sort
4. **Computer** or tablet with **editing capabilities**

THAT'S IT! Told you it was **easy**...

Actually, there's a bit more to it, especially when it comes to **exactly HOW** to get started. So, let's dive into the details.

All YouTube creators work in their **creator studio**. Not a studio IRL but a virtual one, one that's in your YouTube channel account. This is essentially your **backstage area** and it's where all the YouTube creator **WIZARDRY** goes on. This is the place where you upload your videos, and all the other YouTube **'tricks of the trade'** can be managed from here too.

In order to learn all this stuff you need to get **ultra organised**. So, let's make a **PLAN.**

To make the **PLAN** a little easier let me introduce you to one of my YouTube **BFFs, Marvela...**

She's brilliant at making lists and getting organised with video. She can transform what I've been talking about so far into a checklist so you can easily follow along and remember what needs to be done.

Bio

NAME:

Marvela

Specialist knowledge: Checklist extraordinaire

Good points: Very organised

Loves: Singing, dancing and making lists

Favourite YouTube Topics: Comedy, knitting, design singer / songwriters

Hola mis gatitos, I have prepared a purrfect checklist that will remind everyone of what they need to do to **make a fantastic YouTube channel**. (BTW 'hola mis gatitos' means 'hello kittens' in Spanish.)

Follow me...

THE EASY WAY!

Things to take on your YouTube journey

I believe you must try to be **very organised** if you want to be an awesome YouTube creator. So, I would like to share an activity checklist to help you create **your amazing YouTube channel.** I have broken this down into 5 easy steps.

1. Create a plan

First of all, you need to plan out **what videos** you want to create and **how often** you think you will be able to make them. Being **consistent** is an important factor if you are thinking about being a YouTube creator in the future. Being consistent means making and publishing videos on a regular basis. For now, as you're just starting out, publishing your video often is not as important **BUT** learning to **plan your video is super essential**.

See the backstage area (Chapter 8) for your video planner reminder.

2. Make great videos

You never know when a good idea will work on video, so if you don't know I say **HAVE A GO** anyway. Keep experimenting. Keep making videos. See which ones you like making the best and see which ones your community like. **NO IDEA IS TOO CRAZY.**

EXPERIMENT, EXPERIMENT, EXPERIMENT

Think about making videos people will want to watch. For example, do you think viewers would be interested in watching a video of you playing a video game, telling a story or making cupcakes? Compare that with something a bit boring like a video of your pet cat sleeping. Actually, that's not a great example as lots of people love watching sleeping cat videos! **#CatTherapy is a thing. YEAH.** Let me use a better example...how about a video of a grass head plant growing in real time? That would be quite boring as it may take days, if not weeks, to grow. But you could make it more interesting by creating a **time lapse video** instead. That way you can speed up the video so everyone can see how a grass head plant grows.

3. Prepare your equipment & props

A lot of pro YouTubers like moi (BTW 'moi' is French for 'me') have an extra special quality and are **extremely CLEVER** (even if I do say so myself). They often don't have the luxury of lots of equipment and studio space, but this is what makes them very special indeed, and what makes you special too.

The thing about us YouTube creators is that if we don't have all the things we need to make a video we will try to use whatever we can get hold of to make the video happen.

YouTubers know the most important thing is to get the **video recorded, edited and uploaded**. When YouTubers don't have that shiny new tripod or camera, their very special **THRIFT GIFT** (**AKA** being resourceful) kicks into action. Suddenly cardboard boxes become the best adjustable height surface and books have a dual purpose – a great source of knowledge and a perfect camera balancer! Your reading lamp and window light become great **ring light and soft box substitutions**. We make do with what we've got. That's how to get started the easy way.

Glossary: Ring lights and soft boxes are a form of lighting equipment that help video and film makers create effective and desired lighting effects as well as light up a dimply lit set so that a better quality image can be captured.

4. Get your videos found

If you want an audience of frequent viewers for your **amazing videos** you need to get your videos **uploaded and discovered**. This is the stage of building your community of people interested in your video topics.

5. Take plenty of action and practise

HAVE A GO at making a video. It doesn't matter what it is about at this point, it can be literally anything. This is about **getting started**. Film your favourite objects or toys, do a room tour, or just practise talking into the camera, **selfie style**.

Let's sum up

Make a little **plan** as it helps you to stay **organised**, but also let your imagination **run wild**. Go to town with your video ideas. Go crazy (not **BONKERS**, just **crazy**)! **HAVE A GO** at filming your ideas with whatever camera device you have available. Most importantly, just get started and, of course, make sure you have fun. (Somehow I don't think you will have any trouble with the fun bit!)

Check out the table below to get an idea of some of the things you may need to start preparing for making videos and creating a video plan.

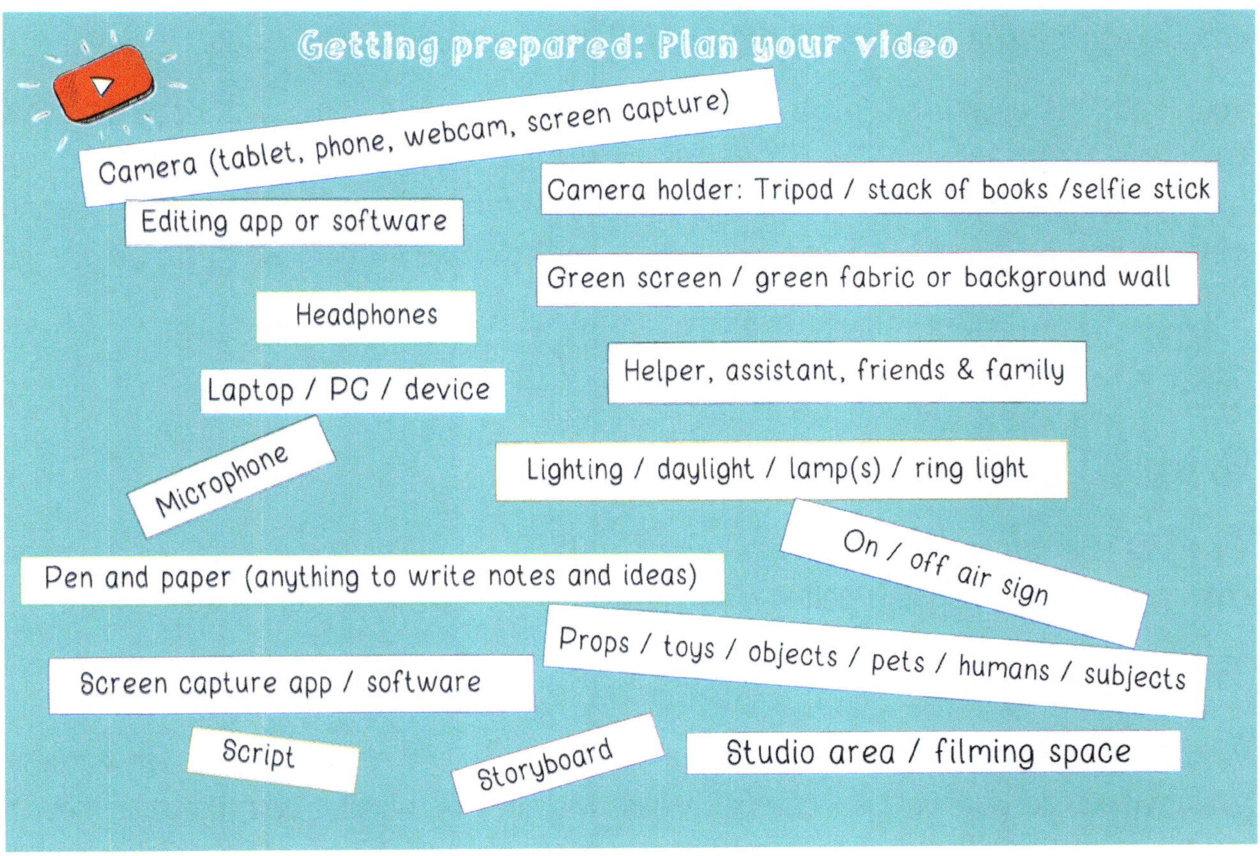

Charlie

Thanks, Marvela! That was super informative and helpful.

Marvela

Thanks, Charlie. Your readers are delightful. So attentive. I'll hand back over to you...

YOUTUBE BASICS FOR SERIOUS BUDDING YOUTUBE CREATORS

Serious YouTuber cats always make sure they have a goal for their channel. This helps create a successful **YouTube career**, if that's what you want to do.

Your YouTube channel is like a reflection of your creative ideas and **represents you and your interests**. If you are serious about being a pro YouTube creator in the future, you may find my looking **GLASS acronym** useful when remembering some important factors that can help make your YouTube channel extra special.

Why GLASS?

GLASS is like a mirror. A mirror – which reflects you when you look at it – is made from glass, hence why it is called a **looking glass.** I thought it quite appropriate!

G stands for GOAL

Why do you want a YouTube channel? (Refer back to the reasons you ticked earlier). What videos do you want to create? What will they be about? Who do you want to create them for? For example, do you want to make videos for fun to share with friends and family? Do you want to make videos to keep as memories for private viewing? Or do you want to make videos about a hobby you do and share that with others who have the same hobby?

L stands for LONGEVITY

Are your videos about subjects that people will want to watch over and over again? For example, a video telling a classic story like 'Sleeping Beauty' or a list of educational facts about space is likely to be **viewed again and again** as they are subjects and stories that people want to learn about and revisit. Sometimes these subjects are called **EVERGREEN** topics, yes just like an **evergreen tree!** On the other hand, a video about a morning routine or a **trending challenge** may only be watched once or for just a short period of time.

A stands for AUDIENCE

Who would you expect to enjoy watching your videos? Are your viewers likely to be the same age as you, or older or younger? At school or college?

Have a think about who your viewers might be and what their interests and hobbies are. Maybe even think about what country they could be from.

This may affect what you say and how you speak to your viewers, so it's always good to consider these things. For example, if you're speaking about the school system in the UK but you have lots of viewers from the US or Australia, you may want to explain what school years equate to in those countries.

S stands for SHAREABILITY

Make videos that people would want to share with others. If you make fun, entertaining and valuable videos, **viewers will want to share** them. These could be in the form of short jokes or videos with an interesting premise. For example, a 'how to' on pet accessories, a new book review, a gaming series, or a funny music video using your

AWESOME talent all have the potential to be shared with others interested in watching.

The key is to make your video the best it can be so that people enjoy it enough to want to share it with their friends and family.

S stands for SUSTAINABILITY

This one is easy. If making videos is not fun or interesting for you, your YouTube channel is **NOT sustainable.** Can you maintain creating videos over a long period of time or will you get bored?

Making videos is great fun and they can be very quick to make once you've had some practise. If you think you might get **bored** easily then a **serious career** making YouTube videos might not be for you. However, you can still practise and **have lots of fun** with it and it's okay if you don't want your channel to be for ever. You won't know until you **HAVE A GO** and see how you feel.

TIPS AND TRICKS:

- **YouTube ain't for the faint.**
- Being a full time YouTube creator requires **creativity** and **commitment**. That's why it's a great idea to practise making videos now. If you decide to follow a video or film making career when you're older, you'll be fully equipped with all the right skills and knowledge. This will make it nice and easy for you to make your dream come true. **This gives home learning a whole new meaning.**

If you're still with me then **CONGRATS** because I know you're serious about making videos.

Stick with me – we've only just covered the basics so if that's already got you **FIRED UP** and you're ready to get your **imagination juices flowing** then you're in for a very exciting **YouTube ride**!

So, what are you waiting for? **Let's get started** and create your channel!

WOO HOO! FOLLOW ME THIS WAY...

HOW TO DECIDE ON YOUR YOUTUBE CHANNEL TOPIC

FOCUS POCUS

Your **YouTube channel topic is the main subject** you would like your YouTube channel to be about.

Some of you may have a **GAZILLION** ideas for your video channel and some of you may have **ZERO.** Pero no problema. (BTW that means 'but no problem' in Spanish.) I'm here to help you **FOCUS on a topic idea** that can help you create the right videos for you. Having **a clear idea about the main topic or category** you want to cover on your channel will inspire more ideas as you go on and help you to keep creating. This will ensure you **stay on track** to having a successful channel, if that's what you want.

WHAT is your YouTube channel about? What topics do you want to cover in your YouTube videos? If you have more than one topic and want to do lots of things on your channel, **which one is the main topic you want to cover**? These are the types of questions you should ask yourself when you're starting to make videos.

See the backstage area (Chapter 8) for your YouTube channel topic ideas list.

If you are already sure of your topic idea, then that's **PURRFECT**. If you're not sure, then to help you discover your topic, answer this: What general YouTube 'category' would you like your videos to fit into?

Here are some examples of topic ideas you may want to focus around:

Checklist: Examples of general video topics

☐ Animals	☐ Environment	☐ Magic tricks
☐ Animation	☐ Fashion	☐ Medicine
☐ Art	☐ Fitness	☐ Music
☐ Beauty	☐ Gaming	☐ Reviews
☐ Computers	☐ Food	☐ Science
☐ Dance	☐ Health	☐ Space
☐ Design	☐ Lifestyle	☐ Sport
		☐ Technology

Another way to think about it is: **What do you want your channel to be known for?**

Here are some examples that may help you. Do you want to be the YouTuber who:

- gives funny commentary and reactions to events and videos?
- creates original T-shirt designs?

- reviews the latest video game?
- creates artistic doodles or designs?
- shows others how to create their own fashion?
- teaches dance choreography for video shorts?
- makes short comedy skits or plays pranks?
- discusses renewable energy and environmental issues?

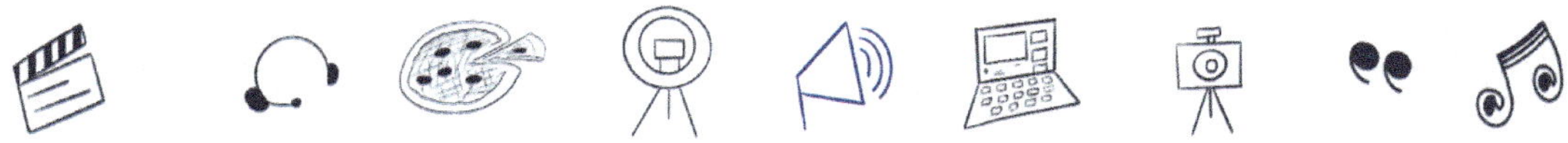

As you can see, there are lots of ideas to choose from and topics to be known for. You may have a clear idea now. If you're still not sure then that's okay too, as that's how most YouTubers start out.

Ted

But how do you decide on a channel topic if you don't have any ideas or have so many ideas that you can't decide which ONE to choose?

Charlie

That's easy...go through these 3 magic doors to find what you really enjoy and what you would most like to create videos about.

Another way to **get some topic ideas** is to do some research to discover what topics are relevant to you. To uncover the mystery of your favourite things and learn more about your personality just...

open the following 3 doors and answer each question:

What themes run through your hang out space?

Look around your bedroom / hang out space. What things and colours can you see? What books, posters, games, gadgets and toys dominate your room? Do you have a theme? Do you have animals everywhere? What are they – pelicans, cats, tigers, apes, hamsters, dogs? Do you have a fascination with space and science or music and performing? Do you have instruments in your room? What else do you have in your space and **what do you love**? Do you have computers, gadgets, electronics, video games, a TV and devices in the spaces that you hang out in most? Do you love the arts, painting, drawing, crafts, model making, dolls' houses, books? Do you have football, soccer, basketball or other sports stuff around?

Aside from all the plushies you still have hanging out in your space, check to see if you can learn something about yourself by examining a theme with the other objects, posters and paraphernalia.

Can you record videos in your space? Does your room or space need a makeover perhaps? Or maybe you just need to clear all that stuff off the floor! I'm pretty sure you will start to see some things around you that reflect what you **LOVE**, what you have always **LOVED** and that you will probably always **LOVE** in the future. You'll be surprised how easily the clues in **your hang out space** tell you about yourself.

Hopefully this exercise has given you some inspiration for **video topic ideas**.

MAGIC DOOR #2

What things do you most <u>enjoy</u>?

What **hobbies** or after school **clubs** do you **LOVE**? What are your **favourite subjects** at school? Who are **your favourite YouTube creators** and what are their YouTube channels about? What are your personal **interests**? What kind of music do you love? What films or musicals do you love and **what do you enjoy** most about them?

It can be very helpful to understand a little more about what you like doing. Sometimes this is obvious, but at other times it's worth answering some of the questions above to help you discover more about yourself and what makes you tick.

MAGIC DOOR #3

What are you good at and how would you describe your personality?

How would you describe yourself? What do your family, friends and teachers say you're good at? Do you agree? If you do, can you use those things to help you get ideas for your channel videos? For example, if your friends and family say you are **funny** you might want to add a comedy element to your videos. Perhaps you could do a channel featuring funny skits or jokes. If you're good at magic maybe you could do magic tricks in your videos. **That sounds fantastically entertaining to me!**

If this exercise doesn't work towards helping you decide on a channel topic and you still can't think of anything, then my **best advice** is to keep brainstorming those ideas and you will eventually have your genius **lightbulb moment**. Even if you have **little sparks of different ideas** then write them down and explore them further.

TIPS AND TRICKS:

- Focus on and experiment with your ideas.
- **HAVE A GO** at making videos on your chosen topic idea. Experimenting with lots of ideas at first is the best way to start. Eventually you will find out which idea is the most fun. You might also find that you need to go from one idea to another before you find the thing you really love.
- If you want extra help deciding what to make videos about, try completing the 'Video Topics Challenge' below. This may help you focus on ideas.

Video Topics Challenge

Tick all the things you would likes to include in your videos

- [ ] Singing
- [ ] Music
- [ ] Video games
- [ ] Acting
- [ ] Pets
- [ ] Animals
- [ ] Comedy skits
- [ ] Pranks
- [ ] Challenges
- [ ] Make-up
- [ ] Hair
- [ ] Fashion
- [ ] Routines
- [ ] Cooking
- [ ] Vlogging
- [ ] Sports
- [ ] Tech reviews
- [ ] Reviews
- [ ] Baking
- [ ] Model making
- [ ] Art
- [ ] Other

Tick the things you think you would like to do or show in your YouTube videos... (tick all the boxes that interest you)

Q&A

Prof. Alga Rhythm

Can I do lots of different topics on one channel?

Charlie

It depends on how similar the topics are. It's better to stick to one main topic and add in a few other related topics. For example, let's say baking is your main channel topic idea. It would be better to add topics related to baking. You could add recipes, taste testing, Bake Off style competitions and even birthday cake decorating. Basketball tips and Minecraft gameplay videos, however, are not related to the main topic so these videos might not be suitable if you wanted to focus your channel on baking. But the odd unrelated topic would also be fine. When you're starting out you may have a mix of different topics until you decide which one you want to focus on.

Marvela

So, I can mix it up a bit? For example, can I mix 'my pet hamster's morning routine' video with a 'how to make a tie-dye T-shirt' video?

Charlie

Yes, you can. Especially while you're starting out and experimenting. However, if you're looking to grow your channel and build a community in the future then it could be a bit confusing for your viewers to see unrelated video topics.

Marvela

So, I should experiment with a few different topic ideas first, find the one that works for me, then stick to that (if I enjoy it of course)?

Charlie

Precisely. Nicely put! If you're looking to be a serious YouTube creator pro in the future, then it is best to focus on one main topic and add videos that fit in naturally with the main topic you have chosen.

WELL DONE!!

You have done amazingly well so far.

I think you're ready to write out your channel plan...

YOUR CHANNEL PLAN

Your channel plan is made up of all the things we've talked about so far, that's

WHY you want a YouTube channel

and

WHAT your channel is going to be on

and

WHO you think will watch your videos.

Your YouTube channel plan is basically how you would **describe what your channel is all about** using the above. Let's do this together.

Your personal 'YouTube channel description':

Example 1:

I want to start a YouTube channel about

(your main topic) the environment

(why) because I care about the future of planet earth and

(for who) I want to help people who care about climate change and are looking for ways to help stop global warming.

(your video ideas) My videos will show simple everyday things that people can do at home which can help make a difference towards improving the environment.

Example 2:

I want to start a YouTube channel about

(your main topic) gaming

(why) because I enjoy playing Minecraft and giving a running commentary of what's going on during my play. I want to share my skills and game play experience

(who) with people who enjoy watching Minecraft and want to get some ideas, learn about Minecraft and generally have fun watching and listening to my commentary.

(your video ideas) My videos will show Minecraft gameplay as well as other video games.

HAVE A GO: CRAFT YOUR OWN CHANNEL DESCRIPTION.

Fill in the blanks below to describe **WHAT** channel you want to start, **WHY** you want to start it and **WHO** will enjoy it.

I want to start a YouTube channel about ________ (your main topic) because I ________________________ (why) for ________ (who) with my videos that show ______________ (your video ideas).

See the backstage area (Chapter 8) for more examples like this and craft your own YouTube channel description.

TIPS AND TRICKS:

Try this to find ideas for your YouTube channel topic:

- Watch 2 of your favourite YouTube channel presenters and write down 3 things you like about their personalities.
- Then pick 2 of your favourite videos and write down what you liked about them.
- What personality traits do you share with these YouTube creators? What general topic ideas do they cover? Do you want to do something similar?
- Imagine how you would like your YouTube channel homepage to look. Have a go at designing your artwork and video ideas.

HAVE A GO: DESIGN YOUR CHANNEL HOMEPAGE.

See the backstage area (Chapter 8) for your YouTube channel homepage template. Sketch out how you want your channel homepage and banner artwork to look and what you want it to say.

Chapter 3

PLAN

CHAPTER 3: PLAN

PREPARING YOUR VIDEOS

As a YouTuber I get lots of questions, mainly about where I get my trainers (or sneakers if you're in the USA) and what my favourite pizza is, but I also get questions about YouTube, like:

- What equipment do I need to get started?
- How many videos do I need to upload a week?
- What should I do about copyright strikes?
- What should I name my channel?

I'm sure you've got lots of questions too, so let's dive into the nitty gritty of getting your channel started!

HOW TO START YOUR YOUTUBE CHANNEL

Let's start your channel with a simple **PLAN** – a road map so you always know where you are, where you are heading and where you want to get to.

REMEMBER! Every 'super tuber' has some kind of plan....

Charlie

Marvela, would you like to explain how to make a plan to easily create an awesome YouTube channel? You can use our pizza example if you want.

Marvela

Perfecto! I'll get straight to it. BTW love the new look, last time I saw you your hair was flat…suits you.

Charlie

Thanks. It's amazing what you can do with a little bit of candle wax. (Please don't try this at home. It takes a lot of skill to create this look!)

I have a **PURRFECTLY AWESOME IDEA!** Sometimes it can be a little confusing and there are lots of things to think about, but the easiest way to create your YouTube channel is to create it in **3 SIMPLE STEPS.** Each step happens in a specific order. Think of it as a **PIZZA**. There are 3 main steps, or layers, to build your pizza. You have the **base**, the **sauce** and the **toppings**. Voilà. (BTW 'voilà' is French for 'there it is'.)

One layer has to sit on another layer to make a delicious pizza. That's what your channel is like. You have your **base layer**, **middle layer** and your **top layer** (and maybe a little olive oil for the more adventurous budding YouTubers out there!).

Let's go through each of your 3 pizza layers, or steps, of your YouTube channel.

THE 3 EASY YOUTUBE CHANNEL STEPS

YouTube Channel STEP #1 THE PLAN: The pizza base layer

Your base layer is the foundation of your pizza. The layer that the rest of the yummy pizza can sit on and stay strong and delicious. Your channel is the same. You need to make sure the **foundation part of your channel** is firm enough to build the other parts of the channel on.

In order to create a firm channel base you need to **set up** your channel, write a **plan** and describe the following:

- **What** you want your channel videos to be about
- **Who** might be interested in watching your videos
- **How** many videos you plan to upload and publish in a month or a year

YouTube Channel STEP #2 YOUR SPECIAL STYLE: The pizza middle layer

Your middle layer is the **core** of your channel. It's the layer that has Mama's special sauce, making it even more delicious. It keeps the base and top layers firmly in place. It's like your **character**. Put some thought into the middle part of your channel. Consider **what goes into making your videos fun**, **entertaining**, **authentic and unique.**

This is really where all the **magic happens**, the ingredients that give you your **special edge** (it's not called secret sauce for nothing!). It could be your style, personality, imagination, talent or your je ne sais quoi. It's your personal stamp, your uniqueness, your flavour, or whatever makes your channel different and enjoyable. (BTW 'je ne sais quoi' is French for 'I don't know what'.)

YouTube Channel STEP #3 VIDEO TOPIC IDEAS: The pizza top layer

Your top layer is of course the pizza toppings. This is the layer that sits on top of the pizza making it super delicious. In terms of your YouTube channel, it's the **creative element and the variety of your video topic ideas and video style.** Your choice of toppings (or topics in the case of your channel) will set you apart from other channels (or pizzas!).

When creating your YouTube channel it's easier to do it in steps (or pizza layers!). **Each step, or layer, has a different function** but they are all **equally important**. When you put them all together you have the potential for a great channel or a perfect pizza complete with Mama's special sauce.

Layer 1
The plan
(The pizza base)

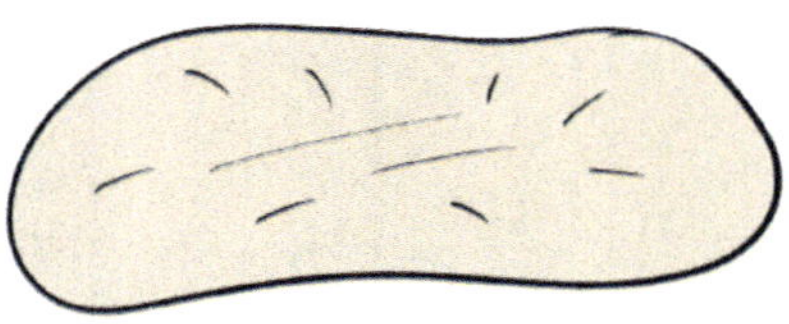

Your channel plan and idea.

Layer 2
Your Special Style
(The secret sauce)

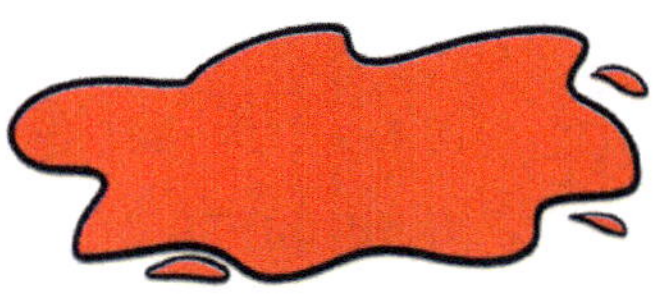

Your special style, unique personality, talent, storytelling or jokes.

Layer 3
Video topic ideas
(Your pizza toppings)

Your choice of video topics.

YUM!

Ready for more?

We've been through the theory, so if you're still serious about being a YouTube pro creator then let's get cracking. Put your seat belts on kids 'cos we're going for a little video ride…

NOW…let's get on to some pizza / video making!

Let's talk about the first layer of your YouTube channel pizza – **the base or the set up**. This is where you give your channel a name and figure out what kind of videos you want to create and upload to your channel. **Let's start with what you want to call your channel.**

HOW TO NAME YOUR YOUTUBE CHANNEL

Cats and kittens, let the creative video making **FUN** commence!

Do you know what you want to call your channel? Your channel name is important as it is what you will be known as for as long as your YouTube channel exists. Coming up with the right channel name is **SUPER IMPORTANT**.

BTW, you can change your channel name if you want to later on. Be careful though as once you have changed your URL, or channel custom URL to your chosen channel name, your URL can't be changed. I'll give you more details on this later on. For now, let's try and figure out a name that you will enjoy having for a long time.

Here's Marvela again to help you with ideas for creating your **awesome channel name**. Marvela, what's next on the list?

So, let's look at Charlie's new channel preparation:

1. **Reason for starting a channel.** Charlie's example: I want to have a YouTube channel because I want to teach as many people as possible how to be a cat so that they can enjoy the wonders of cat life. ✓

2. **Main video channel topic.** Charlie's example: I want to show people how to live a charmed life as a pet cat – the ups, the downs, the ins, the outs, the challenges and the comforts. ✓

3. **Channel name.** Charlie's example: Cutie Pie (because I'm so cute you could eat me). ✓

Charlie

YAY! LET'S GO AND MAKE SOME VIDS!

Marvela

BTW Charlie, did you check that no one else has your YouTube channel name?

Charlie

OH NO, I didn't.

Marvela

Okay, no worries, but it's really important to check that you have a unique name sooner rather than later. For example, let's check if your name idea 'Cutie Pie' is available…

To search your name idea all you have to do is type it into the YouTube search box and check if other YouTube creators already have it. If it's taken, you just have to find another one. Keep searching until you find a channel name that hasn't been taken.

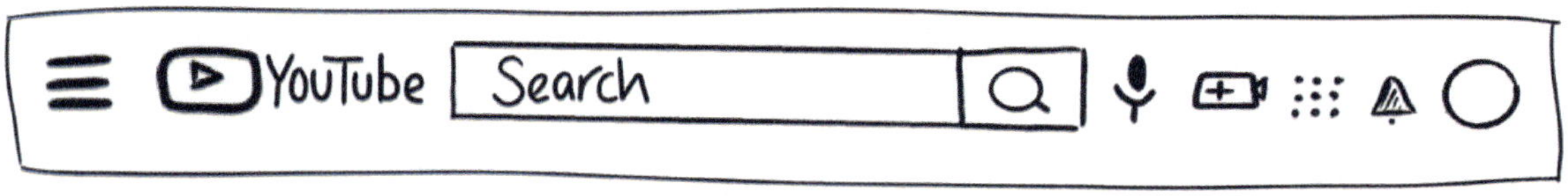

Charlie

SEARCHING: 'CUTIE PIE' – it's **GONE**! How could that name be taken already? I thought I was the only 'Cutie Pie' in the world!

Charlie

SEARCH: 'Cutie Pie with a K' – 'KUTIE PIE' – it's taken too!

Why does **'Kutie Pie'** sound so familiar?

Okay, let's try 'CUTIE PIE 1234' – YAY, IT'S AVAILABLE! But it sounds so 2010. I didn't realise there were so many cats on YouTube – I thought I was the only one!

Marvela

The fact is there are a lot of cute cats out there.

Charlie

SEARCHING: **'CUTIE CAT'**

SEARCHING: **'TALKING CATS & PIZZA'**

SEARCHING: **'DIGITAL CATS EAT PIZZA'**

SEARCHING: **'CAT PIZZA PORTAL'**

RANDOM FACT ALERT

'PewDie Pie' was the world's first independent YouTube creator to reach 100 million subscribers.

Charlie

I've decided to focus my channel around pizza because I LOVE pizza. With that in mind, what do you think about 'CHARLY MAKES PIZZA' or 'CHARLY'S PIZZA HOUSE' for the channel name?

Marvela

Sounds like a great plan Charlie. I like the first one. It's pretty catchy and according to my search it's available. Yay! The second one sounds a bit too much like a pizza delivery service.

How did you come up with '**Charly Makes Pizza**'?

Charlie

Well, I figured I could have my catchy pet name, Charlie with a Y, plus something to describe what my channel is about so that people will know what to expect from my videos. It was quite logical really – I also used my special YouTube naming formula:

CN=MN + CT

CN=MN+CT (<u>C</u>hannel <u>N</u>ame = <u>M</u>y <u>N</u>ickname + <u>C</u>hannel <u>T</u>opic)

(Charly Makes Pizza = Charly + Pizza)

Marvela

That's **GENIUS** and original, I didn't realise it was so easy! You're quite the Einstein.

Charlie

Thanks, I'm a big fan. I've seen nearly all his videos.

I like to stick to a **KISS** formula. When I get in a muddle about anything, whether it's home learning or researching YouTube channel names, I just take a deep breath and say **KEEP IT SIMPLE, SWEETIE**. And the answer suddenly comes to me. Works a treat every time.

RANDOM FACT ALERT

When Einstein was young his teachers didn't think he was very smart. He was even expelled from school. BUT when he was 10 years old he became passionate about MATHS, SCIENCE and PHILOSOPHY and went on to DISCOVER the 'Theory of relativity' and the world's most famous equation $E=MC^2$. This stands for ENERGY equals MASS (matter – basically just stuff to you and me) times the SPEED OF LIGHT squared.

You can be as **creative with your channel name** as you like. Write down some channel name ideas, test them out with friends and family. Which do they like best? Decide which name is your final choice and set forth with your official channel name. Here are some simple channel name examples using various video topic ideas:

- Marvela's Baking Hour
- Sam The Kid Gaming
- Bella's Short Stories
- Monty's Musical Montages
- Aiden's Environmental Vlog

BTW, I've used stage names or nicknames here. You can use your YouTube channel name anywhere on your channel and add it to your channel artwork. You can even get a personal YouTube website address (**AKA your custom URL**) which is basically like your YouTube channel website address. For example, **YouTube.com/CharlyMakesPizza** **or** **YouTube.com/NurseryRhymes** **so** there's no crazy random code, just a nice simple YouTube site address that is easy to say and understand.

Getting your custom URL

To claim your **custom URL** (your personal YouTube website address) YouTube requires your account to:

- have 100 or more subscribers
- be at least 30 days old
- have a channel icon and uploaded channel art

You **CANNOT** edit a **custom URL** once it has been created so **CHOOSE WISELY.**

Glossary: Custom URL. If eligible, you can give fans an easy-to-remember web address, called a custom URL, for your YouTube channel. This will look like: youtube.com/yourcustomname or youtube.com/c/yourcustomname.

TIPS AND TRICKS:

- **REMEMBER** to use a nickname or stage name when creating your channel because it's **important** to always keep your **personal information**, such as your name, age, address, phone number and date of birth **PRIVATE.**
- You could spell your name differently or give yourself a **nickname, pen name or stage name**. All the greats do it and it's a wonderful chance to call yourself something that you like. For example, I call myself **Charly with a 'y'.** Get creative. What nickname would you give yourself?

WHAT VIDEOS SHOULD YOU MAKE FOR YOUR CHANNEL?

YOUR VIDEO CONTENT PLAN

Try and keep your topics related. If your channel is about gaming, have gaming related videos. If your channel is about cooking, have cooking related videos. If your channel is about climate change, have environment and nature related videos. You get my drift.

Glossary: Video content is basically all forms of video you see on the internet. This includes vlogs and animations as well as live and recorded videos. YouTube creators often refer to their videos as their video content.

To get an idea of what video content is, take a look at the following video breakdown:

First let's look at your channel's **main topic**. For example, **PIZZA!**

Sub topics then come **under** the main topic. For example, pizza making in Italy, pizza restaurants, pizza making challenges, making your own doughballs and how to make gluten free pizza. How to play the latest pizza themed video game. These are all sub topics of my main topic **PIZZA**.

You can try any **TOPICS, SUBJECTS OR IDEAS** when you are starting out. You may not have it all figured out when you start, and that's okay. You may think you want to do a channel on one idea but end up focussing on another few ideas. That's **OKAY** too. **REMEMBER!** It'S **YOU**Tube – **YOUR** channel and **YOUR** ideas. The **YOU** is there for a reason. Keep practising and making those videos, **exploring and experimenting with topics** you enjoy or believe in. If you make lots of videos on different topics and they don't fit together on your channel because they are unrelated, you can still keep and store those video ideas for another time, or another channel, or just keep them as keepsakes and **memories.** It's always great fun to look back at your first few videos.

As you probably know yourself, there are already hundreds (if not thousands!) of videos on your favourite subjects and interests on **YouTube**. So, think about how you can **make your videos more interesting** or a little different. Perhaps you can **ADD A TWIST** to your video. Think about how you can **MAKE IT UNIQUELY YOURS**. For example, just for fun, you could tell a joke at the start or end of every single video. This will then become your **signature or motif** which your viewers will come to appreciate and associate with your channel.

TIPS AND TRICKS:

Be uniquely **YOU**. Whatever the topic. Here are some ideas:

- You could have a special catchphrase at the start or end of the video.
- You could choose your favourite colour for your backgrounds.
- You could use a background image or animation that appears behind you.

Think about how you can make it uniquely you, **have fun** with it and be **creative**.

Charlie

Are you ready to move on, make some videos and find out more about videography, cinematography and editing?

Marvela

WOWZERS! They are big fancy words for making little videos.

Charlie

That's all the fun, arty, trick stuff that helps make videos even more special. Anyway, thanks Marvela for marvellous tips on getting our plan together.

Looks like we're at the **3RD and MOMENTOUS step** of your video making pizza layers – **THE TOPPINGS**! Let's move on to making your videos look **COOL AKA ADDING FLAVOUR!**

FOR THIS SECTION WE WILL NEED A VIDEO MAKING PRO, SO LET'S MEET CHERRYBELLE AND MAKE AWESOME VIDEOS!!!!!!!!!!!!!!!!!!!!

Chapter 4
RECORD

CHAPTER 4: RECORD

LET'S GET TO IT.

IT'S TIME...TO HAVE SOME FUN MAKING VIDEOS!

Psst...if you've skipped the first section to get straight to the **good bit**, or you're a **VIDEO** know-it-all already, don't worry I won't tell anyone. I'm just glad to see you here, eager to roll up your sleeves and get stuck into video making. It's *100%* the best bit, IMO.

MAKING VIDEOS

It's time to decide what **style** of video you want to make. To do this, I'm going to introduce you to **Cherrybelle**, one of my video recording buddies. She's going to help me tell you all about the **different styles of video** as well as **everything you need to know about recording your videos**. Not only does she make videos at the drop of a hat, she comes up with ideas at the flick of a switch, so who better to help me explain **the art of great video** making than **CherryBelle**?

Bio

NAME: Cherrybelle

Specialist knowledge: Video recording maverick

Good points: Video flair, creativity, environmentally conscious

Loves: Dancing and donuts

Favourite YouTube Topics: Dance, history and lifestyle

Charlie

Over to you, Cherrybelle...

Cherrybelle

Thanks, Charlie. I'm thrilled to be here and can't wait to help out.

Now that you have chosen your **video topic** and **video content ideas** for your channel, it's time to think about the style or **type of videos** you want to create.

There are many **different ways you can produce your videos** and these are often referred to as video styles or sometimes video types. There are different styles because **videos come in all different shapes and sizes** (just like us cats). They vary in the way they are created and produced, and the final video results can be very different.

Glossary: Video style. The ways in which videos are produced and ideas are conveyed to the viewing audience.

TYPES OF VIDEO STYLES

There are all sorts of ways you can put **your ideas on video**. You don't have to use just one style of video; you can experiment and mix it up by using lots of different styles. The **more you experiment with different styles the more likely you are to find which one you ENJOY USING the most**.

Cherrybelle

Marvela, can we look at your fantastic list of the three different video styles please?

Marvela

No problema. Coming right up Cherrybelle. Here's my video style guide list showing the **three main popular video styles**:

1. Animation
2. Screencast or screen capture
3. Live action

Cherrybelle

Thanks, Marvela. You're a **STAR**!

Marvela

De nada. El gusto es mio. (BTW that's Spanish for 'You're welcome. It's my pleasure.')

CREATING ANIMATION VIDEO

You will need specific apps to help you create your animations. You may also want to use a device tablet and digital drawing pen or a very steady drawing finger.

Let's go through these in a little more detail as I'm sure you want to know more about each one.

1. Animation

If you've got a big imagination (which I'm pretty certain you have if you're reading this book) and **love drawing, designing or creating stories**, this is a perfect style for you to explore.

To create animation videos you'll need some tools of the trade.

Tools of the Trade:

- Drawing materials: paper, pens, pencils, computer, tablet
- Animation apps: for example, FlipaClip
- Animation computer software: for example, ClipStudio Paint or Toon Boom Animation
- Stop Motion: Stop Animator, Stop Motion, A Story Age.
- Motion graphics / movie effects: Vimage, Flikitt.

REMEMBER to ask for permission and supervision from a parent / guardian before downloading apps.

There are several types of animation such as **stop motion, motion graphics, 2D or 3D,** but animation is based on the same frame by frame principles overall.

Glossary: Frame-by-frame animation changes the image in every frame so that when the different frames are put together as one they appear to be moving.

I think you'll be familiar with basic animation such as 2D animation, which is like the simple cartoons you see on TV. For example, Pokémon, Scooby Doo and The Simpsons are 2D cartoon animation. There is also 3D animation which is a much more advanced type of animation used by the big movie makers such as **Disney Pixar** and **Dreamworks**.

RANDOM FACT ALERT

Animation is not new. The **PHENAKISTOSCOPE** and **ZOETROPE** were invented over 150 years ago and were the first devices that gave the illusion of movement and animation. The zoetrope device is like a drum with evenly spaced slits for looking through. A sequence of images showing gradual movements in each frame is placed in the drum. When the drum spins around the images appear as ONE MOVING IMAGE.

If you're keen to try animation, read on to hear Charlie explain further.

How to create 2D animation

This one is close to **my heart** as I love animation and I have been creating it for as long as I can remember. Firstly, to create a **frame-by-frame 2D animation**, you need to draw an image on one frame then continue to create more frames, changing the images very slightly in each frame. When these images are displayed together very quickly you will see how they give the illusion of movement.

Cherrybelle

So fascinating! I love that.

These days you can get simple animation software for your computer. I like Toon Boom and ClipStudio Paint as these are what I've used to make my animation videos, but there are lots of others out there. There's lots of styles you can use, I had the most fun exploring my Manga style animations, although I may have to leave that to the experts.

As I mentioned at the beginning of this book, I used to spend hours creating and drawing in my **flipbook AKA flick books**. These days I also use an **animation app**. There are many amazing animation apps but one of my favourite apps is called **FlipaClip**. All you need to do is create the images and storyboard, and the app creates the animation film for you. **See the backstage area (Chapter 8) for recommended apps and animation software. REMEMBER to always ask for PERMISSION when downloading apps or software.**

HAVE A GO: Make your own animated flip book using the activity below.

HAVE A GO: 3 Easy steps to make your own flipbook animation

1. Make your own flipbook by putting about 12 small pieces of paper together. Each piece of paper acts like one frame. You could use a notebook or sketch pad, or even the corner of a paperback book like this one.

2. Draw a little stick figure like the one below. You can draw anything but make sure each image on each page is slightly different.
3. Flick through it with your thumb. You should see your animation come alive – your images appear as a continuous movement.
See the backstage area (Chapter 8) for a done-for-you animation page.

How to create stop motion animation

Stop motion animation uses real objects with small movements in each frame. You can film a series of videos or take photos. Just put these frames / films together and voilà – you have a finished video of moving objects. Editing all the individual frames together creates the **illusion of movement.**

RANDOM FACT ALERT

Stop motion techniques have been used for OVER 100 years. In fact, it's how the first films were made.

HAVE A GO: 4 Easy steps to make your own stop. motion video

1. Place an object or model (or action figures/toys) at one point of your frame (let's call this **point A**). In this video we want the object to appear as if it is moving by itself from point A to another point (let's call this **point B**).
2. Take a photo of the object or film it for 2-3 seconds.
3. Move your object slightly and take another photo (or film it for another 2-3 seconds). Move the object along in the next photo (film clip) and keep doing this until you have moved your object a little further in each photo, from point A to its final destination at point B. You can have as many or as few photos / frames as you like.
4. Add all your photos or film clips together using an editing app such as **iMovie**, **Perfect Video Movie Maker** or **KineMaster** then **PRESS PLAY**. You can also import these photos into your animation app such as **FlipaClip**. The more frames you use the smoother and longer the final film will be.

Glossary: Editing apps allow you to 'glue' all your photos and film footage together to create your final video.

See the backstage area (Chapter 8) for recommended stop motion and animations apps but make sure you get PERMISSION before downloading apps or software.

Motion graphics

This is a real favourite of mine. Motion graphics is a style of video which uses text and shapes. Although this video style doesn't tell a story as such, you can create lovely designs and **digital video art**, as I like to call it. You can add music and sound too, for added effect. It might be for the more adventurous or arty creators, but it's a really fun way to experiment with video making, design and editing without actually filming anything. It's a great way to play around with **art and design apps**, music, and using your imagination. It allows you to be quite abstract and truly experiment with what you can do. Apps like Stop Motion Studio or PicsArt Animator may help.

Random Fact Alert

The THAUMATROPE is a simple animation toy invented in the VICTORIAN AGE. It is one disc with a different image on either side and is attached with string. When the string is twisted and let go of, the disc flips around quickly and the two different images blur and appear as one.

Silhouette / shadow films

Although not strictly an animation (probably more like 'live action'), **silhouette films** have been entertaining people for many years.

It's a simple and fun way to make effective videos without actually appearing in them yourself. The key element is the use of silhouettes. Take a stencil, model, family member or object (toys/ action figures make great subjects for these) and place them in front of a white paper background (or you could use a white sheet).

1. **Place a lamp** so that it is in front of and facing your stencil or object(s).
2. Position your **camera on the other side of the white paper** (or white sheet).
3. For a more dramatic effect, **turn off the room ceiling light** and keep on your **lamp / light which is facing the stencil / object(s)**.
4. Encourage a **family member or friend to help you move your objects around** and perform a story or double act with you. From my own experience, I have helpers queueing up around the block to help me with these types of videos.
5. **Hit record** on your camera and film away.
6. Your camera will record the moving silhouettes only. The **camera can only see the silhouettes** from the other side of the white paper / sheet.
7. If you don't have any narration or a script during the recording you can just add a voice-over or music (or both) at the editing stage and voilà, you've got another **interesting style of video in the bag!**

HAVE A GO: CREATE YOUR OWN SILHOUETTE VIDEO.

See the backstage area (chapter 8) for stencils you can cut out and use for your very own silhouette entertainment.

What you will see through your camera lens

2. Screen recordings and screen capture (AKA screen cast)

Screen capture software enables you to make a digital recording of your computer screen. You can also record your voice during the recording of your screen (screen capture) or edit a **voiceover** narration during the editing stage after you have recorded your screen.

Screencast tools include **Camtasia (for PC)** and **ScreenFlow (for Mac)**. There are others too, such as **QuickTime Player (for Mac).**

See the backstage area (Chapter 8) for gaming equipment and screen capture apps.

WHEN TO USE SCREEN CAPTURE

Screen recording (**AKA screen casting** and **screen capture**) is a way of recording what you see on your computer screen. It's great to use if you are planning on making **reaction**, **gaming** or **tutorial videos** where it's necessary to show your screen.

Gamers make videos by recording and talking through their gameplay. Some YouTube creators play alone and some play with friends. The type of video they typically create is a screen capture recording of their gaming screen. We'll get on to how to do this in a bit more detail in the next chapter, so hang in there all you budding **GAMING YouTubers**.

3. Live action

This video style includes **filming people, objects or scenery**.

It's great way to communicate and **get your message across directly, for tutorials, vlogs, reviews, documentaries, dramas and storytelling**, or entertaining viewers with **music, comedy and just about anything**.

For example, you can present a number of different topic ideas in a live action video. You may want to do **a direct to camera video** to talk about or teach a hobby, explain a challenge, do a skit, present your drawing skills, create dance routines, play an instrument or sing – or all of them if you're feeling ambitious!

How to record live action videos

Find a clear, uncluttered space with **natural light** for best results. Make sure you have all your props in the **camera lens view**. Think about the different shots you want to take. If you are talking directly to the camera, think about positioning yourself in the **middle of the frame**. Do you need to record close ups, or do you need to fit a lot of items or a large area into the frame? Set up your recording space and do some test filming to see what your composition looks like or what things are included in your camera frame. See backstage (Chapter 8 for your composition viewfinder)

Filming using horizontal video (AKA landscape)

Record your video using the horizontal viewfinder. I find this works a treat **for YouTube channel videos**. However, the vertical viewfinder can reduce the quality of your film and you can't fit in as much action as the sides of your film are cut off.

Filming using vertical video (AKA portrait)

A more recent trend has been to record **vertical videos** which just means you record using the **portrait mode**. You'll typically see this on platforms such as **TikTok or Instagram Reels**. They show video clips of peeps doing skits and dances to **pre-recorded music** and **sounds** in portrait mode / vertical film. This form of entertainment and video style is certainly a huge trend that's here to stay, and it works well for short and quick video clips.

The great thing about these platforms that use vertical video is that you can **make and store videos very easily,** so it's a great way to **practise your video making skills** and explore all the different filters and **edit** features.

Ask your parent(s) / guardian(s) to check the minimum age requirements for account users for these platforms. If you are using them to make little videos for practise then you can keep your videos on **private** until you reach the minimum age requirements, but please ask an adult to check the platform rules.

REMEMBER, ONLINE SAFETY IS IMPORTANT!

If you want to transfer **vertical videos** you may have made on another platform, you can download all the video clip files, edit your best vertical videos together, and make one long video of about 5-10 minutes. You can then add this to your YouTube channel (if you feel it fits in and is relevant to your channel topic, of course).

YouTube have introduced their own version of vertical videos called **YouTube Shorts**. No, not the kind that fit on your body! You can make vertical videos up to 60 seconds long and you can add them to your YouTube channel. I haven't tried these myself yet but looks like vertical videos are a fun way to get used to turning your ideas into quick and easy videos.

How to start creating live action videos.

Tools of the trade:

- Any camera
- Peeps / subject or objects
- An idea
- A storyboard
- A script

TIPS AND TRICKS:

Decide on the type of video style you want to use and decide in your mind **which video style fits best for your video idea.**

REMEMBER, ONLINE SAFETY IS IMPORTANT

If you are filming friends or family always ask their permission to record before filming and always tell them what you are going to do with the final film recordings.

How to make AWESOME videos

I hear ya – you've got **your idea** and **your video style** in mind and now you just want to know how to become a total **VIDEO NINJA**!

THE TRICK IS TO GET ORGANISED AND THE TIP IS TO PLAN AHEAD

Congratulations on reaching another **REALLY FUN BIT**. Let's focus on **making fantastic videos** for your YouTube channel. It's been fun so far, Cherrybelle. It's been a **BLAST**! **You certainly know your stuff.**

In my mind, making your videos is the **BEST BIT** of everything, so get comfy as we're likely to stay here for a while.

Tools of the trade:

OK **crazy cats**, let's get started. You will need the following:

1. A piece of plain paper (I'm sure you have some paper lying around), or you could use a whiteboard app).

2. Pencil or pen (the choice is yours, my friend).

Marvela

Wow, I thought making videos was going to be a bit more complicated than that.

Cherrybelle

Well, this is just the start. There's plenty of **video magic** to come. All will be revealed as we go. BTW Charlie, what happened to your hair?

Charlie

Have my fringe spikes fallen again? (BTW 'fringe' means 'bangs' for our USA cats.) My fringe has a mind of its own. I think these camera lights are melting my hair wax. I quite like this look actually. I think it suits me. I think it make me look anime cool. What do you think?

Every great YouTube video starts with a great plan and every great plan starts with a great video maker.

Ted

Nice one, Charlie. Who said that?

Charlie

It's one of my own quotes, drawn from my own experience. Nothing like a bit of **trial and error** to get a plan together complete with **LIGHTS, CAMERA, ACTION**. It always helps our video making projects work like a well-oiled machine.

HOW TO PLAN YOUR AWESOME VIDEOS

There are always lots of things to think about when making great videos, but the real magic starts when **planning** out your video. Your **PLAN** is the special place where you write everything down so you can easily remember **what you need to do as you record your videos**. You can change things as you go as I'm pretty sure you will have all sorts of **fun and crazy ideas**.

This **video plan will help guide you** and make sure you don't forget the important bits to record. When making a video you will need to think about the following parts:

- your video idea
- how to storyboard your video
- creating scenes
- creating a script for intros/outros/main video
- what recording equipment and props you will need
- what, if any, editing requirements are needed (such as special effects, filters and transitions)

Create and plan your video masterpiece

You've probably heard of a **story map**, right? Your teachers may have taught you to create a story map before you write a story at school. It's the same for video. For every video, like every story, you need a **beginning, middle and end**. This helps you end up with a fantastic video! **Am I right or am I right**?

Video Making Planner

You're probably thinking I talk a lot about **planning**, but quite frankly your video planner is like **GOLD**. Take a look at the video planner below and take action for all 6 areas, checking them off as you go. Then you'll know you're ready to grab the camera and start creating your video.

HAVE A GO: PLAN YOUR VIDEO.

See the backstage area (Chapter 8) for your video making planner poster.

VIDEO STORYBOARD & SCRIPTING

Start your video making by creating a **storyboard. DEFINITELY NOT to be confused with story bored!** Storyboarding is a great way to set out what's going to happen in your video. It serves as a **reminder of the scenes you need to film** at the recording stage and also **highlights the equipment** you may need.

Most importantly, creating a storyboard, however long or short, keeps your **video fun and interesting** for your family, friends and fans to watch. It's just like writing a **brilliant book** (like this one!).

How to make a video storyboard in 3 easy steps:

Step 1. Create clear sections

The beginning

The first part of your YouTube video is very important. You need to decide what you **want to say at the beginning of your video** and how you want to introduce the video topic. Think about the things you want to say and show in your video – what can your viewers expect to see?

The middle

What happens in the middle of your video? What's the **main information / content you want to get across** to your viewers? How many scenes do you want to have in the middle part of the video? What do you want to say or show in each scene? How do you aim to you keep your viewers interested?

The end

How do you want to end your video? Is it with the finished results of what you were making, the final thought of the day, or a video recap? There are so many ideas but the key is to end with an interesting conclusion or a summary. As mentioned in Chapter 3, you could have a signature sign-off that is uniquely yours. For example, you may always end with a funny joke or fun fact about your video, or you could even end with a blooper.

Step 2. Sketch out your idea

All you need to do is draw the number of boxes you think you will need and **sketch out what you would like to see happen in your video**. For example, the simple way to do this is to **split up your storyboard into 3 box sections**, like this and sketch out what you would like to see.:

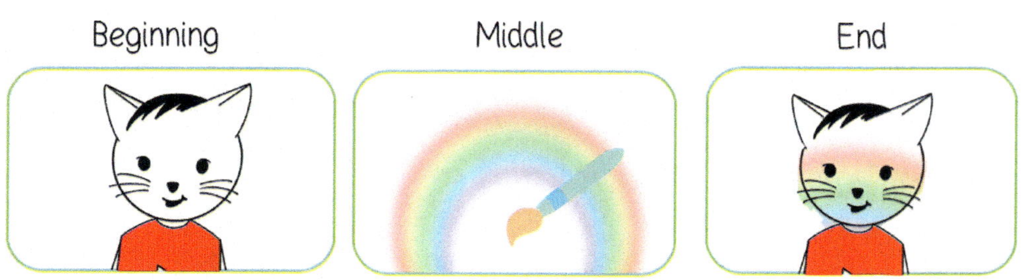

Step 3. Write descriptions for each section

Under each section box, write a brief description of what you want to see happen, in the **beginning**, **middle** and **end** of your video, like this:

Description for beginning scenes	Description for middle scenes	Description for end scenes
I am going to show how I turned into a rainbow cat	I show you how I use rainbow face paint to transform myself into a rainbow cat	I show you the end result of my face painting efforts

Then expand on those ideas a bit, adding more detail to each section.

How to create intros, outros and video scripting

Intros

You are probably well aware of how **YouTubers** introduce themselves and their channels. **Intros** are helpful to have, especially for **new viewers** who have come across your channel for the first time. Over time, as you become more advanced in video making, you can create a script for your intro video and **tag this clip onto each new video you make**. For example, your intro could include a voiceover and logo graphics, or some music, film and text This saves a lot of time when recording videos but, of course, you can always create a quick intro to each and every video as you record them.

Outros

At the end of your video, it's a good idea to guide your viewers to your **other videos on your channel** so they can continue to enjoy **your awesome content.** You can suggest they watch another one of your videos that might be related to the one they have just seen. And don't forget to **remind them to subscribe, like, comment and share.**

Scripting

Scripts are very useful in guiding you through your video topic. The best thing about scripts is that they are very quick and easy to create. They can include as much or as little as you want, but it's a good idea to **keep it simple.** Write a few bullet points that cover the key messages you want to talk about in your video. It's always helpful to **have a script so that you don't forget what you want to say when the camera is rolling.**

Scripts can be especially helpful for your **video intros and outros too**, especially when you are just starting out as a **YouTube creator** or **practising making videos.** Not only do scripts help you when you're filming but they **increase the quality of your video** by giving it a great flow. Additionally, your **viewers get a great viewing experience.** I'm sure you've got some great ideas as to how you would introduce your videos, but if you're stuck take a look at these example scripts:

Intro script

"Hi, welcome to my **YouTube** channel, I'm going to show you how to..."

"So, let's get started!"

I'm sure you've all heard an intro like that before but having a written script **works very well in helping you get started confidently,** and it helps the viewer know what to expect in the rest of your video.

Outro script

"Please subscribe if you want to see more videos like this."

Or

"Check out my other videos about..."

Again, you've probably heard lots of **YouTube creators** say things like this in their outros but you can **create a script that makes it uniquely your own**. Add jokes or pet names for your viewers, for example: **'Welcome back Cutie Pies', 'Thanks for watching my Feline Friends, see you next time' or 'Welcome my Money Honeys'**. (As an added extra, you can personalise your outro style by ending with a pre-recorded funny sound, motion graphics or cool music jingle.) There are some cool apps that can help create quick intros too. Check out Chapter 8 for recommended apps.

In addition to the intro and outro scripts, **consider writing scripts** or list out some points you want to discuss **for each individual part or scene of your video (the beginning, middle and end)**. This helps you remember what you want to say and what to include during your recording.

HAVE A GO: CREATE A STORYBOARD.

See the backstage area (Chapter 8) for your done-for-you planner and storyboard. I have designed it so that you can easily sketch and write your ideas, script and video outline including intros and outros. HAVE A GO at planning your videos!

RANDOM FACT ALERT

Did you know that VIDEO means 'to see / view' in LATIN?

RECORDING A LIVE ACTION VIDEO

Filming and recording equipment

I know you probably think you need expensive phones or cameras and editing software to make **YouTube videos like the pros**, but trust me you don't need drones, Go-Pros, Gimbles or a carload of fancy camera equipment. That's just a **MYTH** and totally **NOT the case**, especially when you're just starting your video making journey.

Marvela

Well, that's a relief otherwise most peeps would never start. What's a **myth** anyway?

Charlie

A story that is believed but not actually true **IRL.**

Cherrybelle

Ah like **FAKE NEWS**.

Tools of the trade:

To **start recording your YouTube videos** you will need a camera – **any camera or recording device**. It doesn't have to be **FANCY.** The recording equipment you need depends on **what style of video you want to make.** For a straightforward film like a vlog you can use a smartphone, compact camera, tablet, or anything else that you can record from (which, let's face it, is **most things these days!**).

Charlie

You're right, it is most things. I recently heard that some spectacles and **toothbrushes come with built-in cameras**, and some even have built-in video games.

Marvela

Surely not!

Charlie

JK on that last one, I made that up. But **TBH** who wouldn't want to play **video games** whilst brushing their teeth, hey?!

Cherrybelle

Thanks guys, shall we get back to it?

If you wanted to make a **different kind of video**, such as an **animation or gaming video, you will need special apps** as these types of videos do not need a traditional camera device. For **animated videos you will need to get ANIMATION software**. For **GAMING VIDEOS you will need screen capture software.** Always make sure you know what type of video you want to make and write a list of all the equipment and apps you will need to **GET READY for the video creation**. Go to the **video style and equipment checklist** for a list of things you may need.

Let's take a close look at what you'll need if you choose to make a **LIVE ACTION** video.

RECORDING EQUIPMENT

1. Filming device: **camera,** tablet, smartphone. Any **digital camera, recording device or smartphone will work**. As you become more advanced you can upgrade your camera or equipment.
2. Tripod and / or use a stack of books to balance your camera.
3. **Lighting**: a good window with lots of daylight or a lamp. You can get a ring light or studio lights (**AKA** softboxes) as you become more proficient.
4. **Microphone**: use your device / PC's mic which is great for gaming / tutorial / review videos. You can use a webcam and a special professional mic as you become more advanced.
5. **Back drop or green screen**: this forms part of your filming set. What are you going to have in your background? What do you want your viewers to see? Try and make sure your background is tidy or find a plain wall as your backdrop.

If you're in a shared space make sure you are not filming family members or friends or even frenemies. Pets are allowed in most cases, but you may want to **seek permission** from the pet owner, not the pet. If you want to use a green screen, you can buy a **special green screen**. But you can easily use green bedsheets or buy some green felt from your local fabric shop, and clip that up in the **background**.

Charlie

Hands up if you have green bedsheets?

Marvela

I don't think it's common to have green bedsheets, Charlie. But next time you order some home furnishings such as blinds or curtains, it's worth thinking about **doubling up – 2 for the price of 1. Get those green sheets ordered in!**

RECORDING YOUR GAMEPLAY

Equipment needed to make gaming videos:

1. Screen capture software: If you want to record your game play using your computer or tablet then you will need some kind of **SCREEN CAPTURE software that records your computer screen which is TOTALLY AWESOME**.

If you want to **record gameplay videos** then you can use special software such as Streamlabs OBS (Open Broadcaster Software).

Glossary: Video streaming. Video broadcasting in real-time – not recorded but being broadcast at the time you are watching.

Charlie

I thought OBS was only used for **streaming** video. I didn't realise it could record video too.

Cherrybelle

Yes, that's right. **Streamlabs OBS** does both. You can use it for live streaming on places like Twitch and recording your gameplay on your computer, which you can edit and turn into a pre-recorded video. It's free and easy to use after your initial set up. Download it and record away, it's pretty cool!

Charlie

Sounds a bit complicated to me. Would this be a perfect time to get your parent(s) or guardian(s) involved to help with the set up set up?

Cherrybelle

Yes, Charlie. You could also play a game together with your parent(s) and record it. Collabs of this kind are all the rage **ATM** and make for an exciting game play video.

BTW you can also record your gameplay on other devices. Let me continue and give you a few pointers in case you want to explore further.

You can also **capture a video of your screen by using the built-in Xbox Game Bar** on Windows computers. Although the Xbox Game Bar records clips of video games, you may need to find other ways to record your voice if you are doing commentary at the same time.

You can **also use Camtasia and ScreenFlow recording software** to capture your screen and either **edit within these apps** or export and edit in your editing software.

Consoles: Xbox and PlayStation.

Make sure you have your controller and USB storage drive ready to store your gaming footage. If you're using an Xbox, connect your USB drive. To capture your screen, go to Settings, Preferences, Broadcast & Capture, Capture location, then SELECT your USB storage drive (it should show up if you've connected it).

If you're using a PS4 copy your game play file from the Capture Gallery to your USB storage drive/device.

Smartphones and tablets: If you're using a smartphone, check out what screen recording apps work on your device. There are a number of apps that can record your device screen.

If you're using a tablet, for example an iPad, you can use the in-built recording app. If you're using an android tablet, check the app store to see what the latest screen recording apps are.

2. Headphones: You can use headphones with or without built-in microphones. The choice is yours. You could start out with regular headphones and use your computer mic or a separate mic. As you get the hang of it, you can upgrade to headphones with a mic.

3. Webcam: Being on camera isn't essential for gaming channels, but if you plan to film yourself while playing your game you can begin by using your built-in device or computer cameras. (You can shrink your video footage of yourself and place in the corner of your game play). Most devices have perfectly adequate quality. However, you may want to invest in a webcam if you plan to use it more often and as you become more advanced in making gaming videos. If you want to appear in your videos **don't forget to get permission from your parent(s) or guardian(s) first!**

4. Gaming chair: Definitely **not essential** to make gaming videos but makes the

experience extra special and increases your gaming performance apparently. I've always wanted one of these chairs. **They look so comfy**. It's still a **DREAM** to be realised so I'll keep you posted on my progress...

TIPS AND TRICKS:

- Start slow, **have a go**, enjoy your gameplay and make sure your friends / family watch your gaming videos.
- When it comes to length, go for a short to mid length gaming video of around **10-20 minutes** when you're starting out.
- If you're on camera then keep your **background area tidy** so it doesn't distract your viewers from the video. And use **background lights** such as a lamp, fairy lights or **LEDs** for that extra special touch. Personally, I always find **neon lighting adds to the gaming atmosphere and aesthetic.**

See the backstage area (Chapter 8) for recommended equipment, apps, software and links.

RANDOM FACT ALERT

People use YouTube to find out how to learn new skills that they have NEVER tried before.

Cherrybelle

Marvela, can you show the smart table that you designed? It makes it nice and easy to decide which equipment we need for the different styles of videos.

Marvela

Yep! Got the video style and equipment checklist table right here:

Checklist: What you need to create different styles of video

Live action film	Animation	Gaming
☐ Any camera device	☐ PC / Phone / tablet device	☐ Screen capture app
☐ Daylight / Lights / lamp	☐ Animation app	☐ Headphones
☐ Background wall / green screen	☐ Steady drawing finger / graphics pen	☐ Microphone
☐ Clear space/ Studio space		☐ Webcam
☐ Props /desk /objects		

See the backstage area (Chapter 8) for your checklist.

TIPS AND TRICKS:

- Be **authentic** in your videos. Don't try to be your favourite influencer, pop star, sports star or YouTube creator, just **be yourself**. Your **FFFs** (friends, family and fans) want to see **YOUR** talent and creative ideas. They want to hear what you have to say and see the way you do things.
- Experiment making different styles of video so that you can find out which you like best.

Glossary: Authentic. Adjective. Of undisputed origin and not a copy; genuine.

STORAGE SPACE

There's only one message on your device that's worse than '**low battery**' and that is '**no storage available**'. Filming anything takes up a lot of space so while recording on tablets and smartphones is quick and easy, it can be very disappointing when you run out of space and get a 'no storage' message.

I know the feeling. It's particularly annoying when I'm just getting into a great recording flow.

Like Charlie, I'm pretty sure that most of you budding video creators have experienced your device's storage running out while recording.

But you don't need to let that stop you from recording your videos. The easy solution to this is to **transfer your film clips or photos** to a laptop, computer or the cloud, or a separate **USB** stick or storage drive.

Always **ask a parent / guardian** to help you store your recordings as they will know the best digital folder to use for your favourite video clips and photos. You will need to know where your videos folder is for when you're ready to edit.

Another way around limited storage space is to use a **dedicated digital camera** for recording videos. **YouTube pros** tend to use compact (small cameras) or **DSLR** digital cameras (big fancy cameras with detachable lenses) for their main **YouTube videos**.

You don't have to use a high tech or fancy digital camera. **Start with a small compact camera**. The great thing about digital cameras is that you can **record large amounts of video** on a dedicated camera using **SD cards**.

Q&A

Marvela

What are **SD** cards?

Cherrybelle

Good question. SD cards are awesome little cards that fit into your digital camera and store all your high quality video clips and photos. You can get them in all sizes. You can easily transfer your video footage to your computer for editing too.

Marvela

What does SD stand for?

Cherrybelle

Another good question. But I don't know. Charlie, can you do a quick search please?

You can get different types of SD cards with different storage capacities which just means some have good storage sizes and some have mega storage sizes. This means you will probably be able to record lots of videos without running out of storage too quickly.

Marvela

BUT what if your SD card does run out of space?

Cherrybelle

Then, all you need to do is delete any film clips on your SD card that you don't want any more, or that you have stored and saved elsewhere. If you don't want to delete your film clips but still need space then you can easily replace your SD card with a brand new one and continue recording. A much cheaper option than buying a new device!

Charlie

SD stands for secure digital. That's what I buy with my birthday gift vouchers. I always like to stay prepared for every eventuality.

TIPS AND TRICKS:

- Check to see if your **family** (including **extended family**) have any **compact cameras** they're happy to let you use. You can export your video clips from the SD card and edit them on a computer or laptop. Different cards store different amounts of video and they are very affordable.
- Involve your parent(s) or guardian(s) in this process so they can help you set up your camera and storage folders. **BIG TIP Remember to label your video files well.**

Sounds like a great plan to me. My aunt gave me her **old digital compact camera** for my birthday as she said she never used it. It's been brilliant. **Shout out to my Aunt Catsby. Nice one!**

Lighting

Lighting is essential for creating great quality videos. **TBH,** all you really need is a **good window** to start. Always aim to have the **window light facing you** as this will be your **main source of light**. The **camera and window** should be opposite to **you or the subject / object** for the best filming results. **Window light is one of the best sources of light** and works wonders for filming. I recommend **filming during the day** as you've probably noticed that not much light comes through windows at night, unless you have a **FULL MOON** shining directly through your window. Actually, that might make for a pretty cool effect!

If you film in the evening when it gets dark you can use a brilliant invention – **the electric light bulb!** Although your ceiling light will work, it's likely to be too dim to get a good quality film recording. In order to better light up your subject(s) / object(s), it's best to use extra lamps in front of you and around you or your subject, making sure they are not in the camera view of course. Assign one lamp as your main light source.

As you progress with making videos you might want to get **small box lights** or some cheap film studio **LED lights (or softboxes)**, which should easily do the job.

Using **fairy lights in the background adds a nice soft lighting effect**. A small amount of **LED lights** in the distant background can also add a fun element to your video's look and feel as it adds a sense of space and texture.

However, if you have lots of multi coloured **LED strip lighting** in your room they can cause a flickering effect so **always do a test video when using various lights before you record your full video.** If they do flicker, switch them off and only use them in a distant background where they don't interfere with your camera.

Ring light, studio lights & day light

If you're recording **gaming videos** and want to have a good quality thumbnail video of your face during the gameplay you can face a window with daylight. However, if you don't have a window, you can **use a webcam light or a lamp to make your videos look clearer**, so long as you place your extra light in front of you. More often than not, your screen lights will light up your face but an extra light will **make your gaming videos look a little slicker.**

If you're doing a **LIVE ACTION video** such as a **vlog or tutorial, a ring light will help light up your face evenly.** Again, if you don't have one you can easily use a table lamp or a window with daylight. There's **no need to get expensive lighting equipment** when starting your channel.

If you are filming a wide space then you may want to place yourself / video subject(s) / object(s) in front of a big window, set up in a garden, or invest in some **studio LED lights**. For now, I recommend using **day light**. **There's lots of it and it's free!**

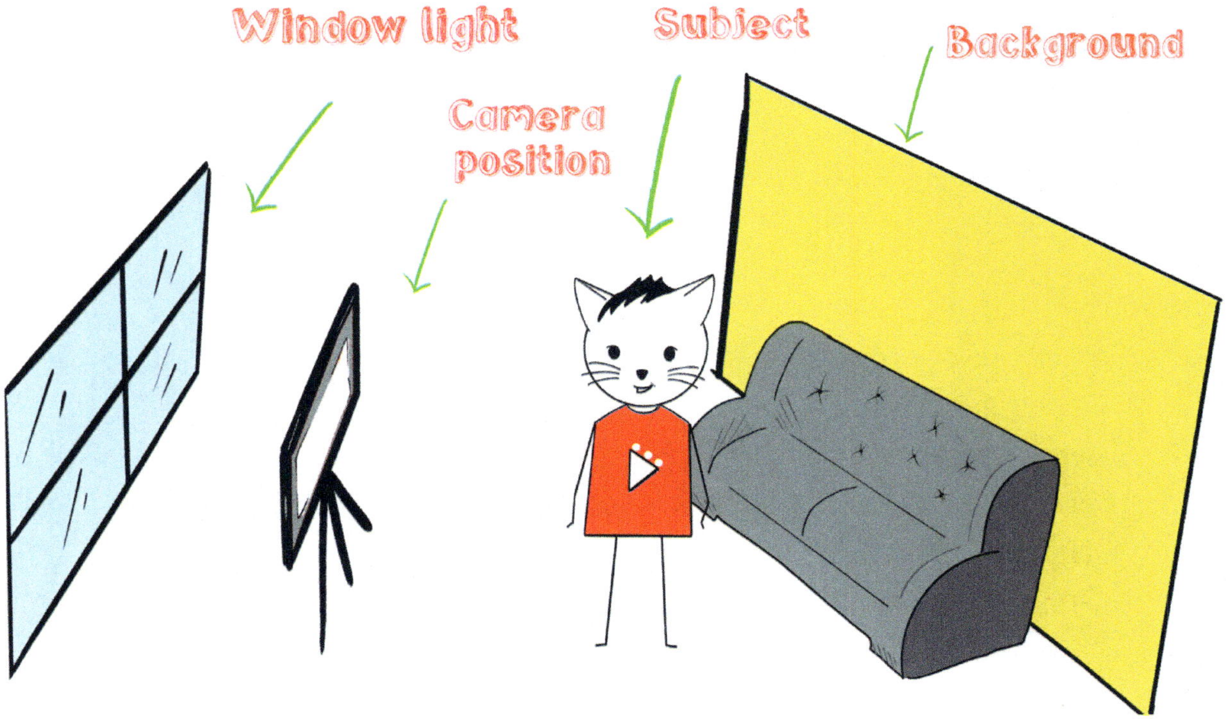

Prepare for filming:

1. Find a space near a window

2. Place the camera at the window end

3. Make sure the camera is pointing towards you or your object(s) / subject(s)

4. Make sure you or your object(s) / subject(s) is facing the window

TIPS AND TRICKS:

- Battery powered **fairy lights are fun, inexpensive and safe to use** and add a lovely touch to your video backgrounds.
- Always try to use daylight if you can. It will light up that gorgeous face of yours and you won't need extra space for studio lights or money for lighting equipment. Even the very best videographers love to use daylight. Studio lights, ring lights and general lamps can create great effects and add drama to your videos.

SOUND AND AUDIO

Most cameras have good quality mics nowadays so you don't need one when you are just starting out. So long as you speak loudly and clearly your camera device should pick up your voice. **REMEMBER to do a few voice warm ups, or sing a favourite song twice before you start recording.** This really helps even out your voice and removes any croakiness. Never underestimate the **power of your voice**. Good, clear audio adds a lot to the quality of your video.

Eventually, as **you become a pro video maker**, you may want to save up some money to buy an external mic so that your **voice sounds nice and clear and smoooooooooooooth.** External mics are available for most devices, including tablets, smart phones, computers and cameras. You can easily plug them into your device if you would like to create a higher quality sound for your video.

Mics can also help reduce that **unwanted fuzzy sound** you sometimes get when using your device mic.

TIPS AND TRICKS:

- **Watch out for unwanted background noises** as you don't want to keep re-recording the same bit over and over.
- Do what you can to **block out** any unwanted background noise. Make sure your windows and doors are shut. This **helps block out background noises** such as chatting / activities, barking dogs and lawnmowers. You get my drift.
- You could also **soundproof** your recording area. If the majority of your surroundings are very hard, such as wooden, marble or concrete floors or walls, it can give your sound an echo. To help avoid this and **improve the sound quality**, record in a well-furnished and carpeted space, or find some blankets, rugs or cushions to lay around your recording space. **Soft furnishings absorb unwanted sound which reduces echo and increases sound clarity.**

STUDIO SPACE

Your **YouTube channel** provides you with your own virtual '**creator studio**' which is private to you. So, when it comes to creating your videos at home, I recommend **creating a little area you can designate to recording videos** and calling it your 'home YouTube creator studio' or 'home YouTube space' or 'video recording studio'.

It's important to think about **setting up an area so you can focus on recording** without getting disturbed. Have you got a small corner of your home you can use for filming without getting in anyone else's way, and where no one (or pets) will intrude, unless they happen to be your video subject(s)? **Think about how much space you may need for you, your equipment and any props too.**

Think about setting up a **mini studio in a chosen space**. If you have to share the space, make sure you can **easily pack your equipment away** after filming and store it safely.

Tell your family when you're starting your video so you don't get interrupted while recording.

And don't forget to tell them when you've finished recording so they can enter the room again.

TIPS AND TRICKS:

- Find a mini studio space that you can set up and call your own during the filming of your videos.
- Having **unwanted guests appearing** in your background can be inconvenient and distracting for your viewers so try to find a quiet space.
- Place a **recording status note** on the door or box around your recording area. You can make your own sign with your own special message, for example: **ON AIR or RECORDING IN PROGRESS or TELEPORTATION ZONE – DO NOT ENTER, or ZAPPED ZONE AHEAD!** This should **HALT** anyone from entering your **FILM SET** while recording is in progress.
- If you're sharing the space with others, be considerate and **don't HOG the space** all day.

See the backstage area (Chapter 8) and grab your ON AIR and OFF AIR video recording status signs or make your own.

GREEN SCREEN

Recording your video with a green background allows you to replace your background later with another image when you are in the editing stage. For example, you can replace the green space in your video background with any picture or video footage that you want. It's really quite fun! Let me show you how you can **HAVE A GO**.

Glossary: Green screen. This refers to the coloured background or object you want to make transparent before replacing it with another image or alternative video footage for the final version of the video.

Q&A

Marvela

What is a green screen?

Cherrybelle

Green screen is an effect that allows you to **replace the background in your video recording** and insert another image. It is replaced at the editing stage of your video and is often referred to as **'chroma keying'.** Our lovely Ted will tell you more about green screen editing later.

Charlie

Do I need a green screen to make YouTube videos?

Cherrybelle

I get this question a lot. No, you don't need a green screen to make videos.

However, if you're thinking about creating a video where you want to change the background then it's a great way to be creative and different and, most of all, have fun with video making and all its splendours.

How to set up a green screen

All you need to do is set up a **GREEN SCREEN** behind you or your video subject(s) / object(s). This can be a simple piece of green fabric, felt or old sheets. (**WARNING:** always ask permission to use and cut up green coloured bedding or clothing!!!)

You can clip or hang a plain green piece of fabric over the back of a chair and sit in front of it with the camera facing you or your object(s) / subject(s). Always make sure your green screen is flat and doesn't have creases. Check out the image below to see what I mean. (You can use lamps or studio lights if you don't have a window, or even in addition to a window). Don't wear a green T-shirt (as Charlie is!) unless you are intending to create some interesting effects. Read on to find out more.

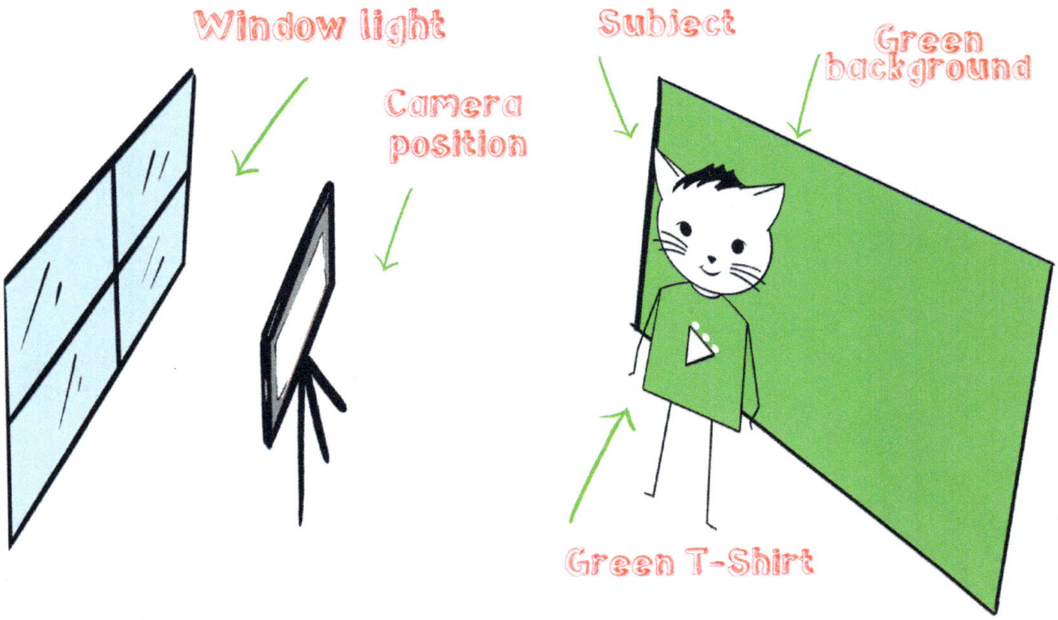

Test your set up by recording a quick video short. This should give you a good idea of what it will look like before you record your longer video.

Charlie

That's so exciting! **Can we make an invisibility cloak** if I wore the green fabric as well?

Cherrybelle

Yes, why not? Let's have some fun and **HAVE A GO**!

All you need to do is get some green fabric or green coloured clothing and make a green cloak to fit around your shoulders. Fasten it at the neck and all the way down the front, or use a green jacket and wear a green T-shirt underneath. The **SECRET** is to wear the colour green anywhere on your body that you want to be invisible in the video.

Record yourself or your object(s) / subject(s) with a green cloak, against a green background. Have a look at this image with Charlie.

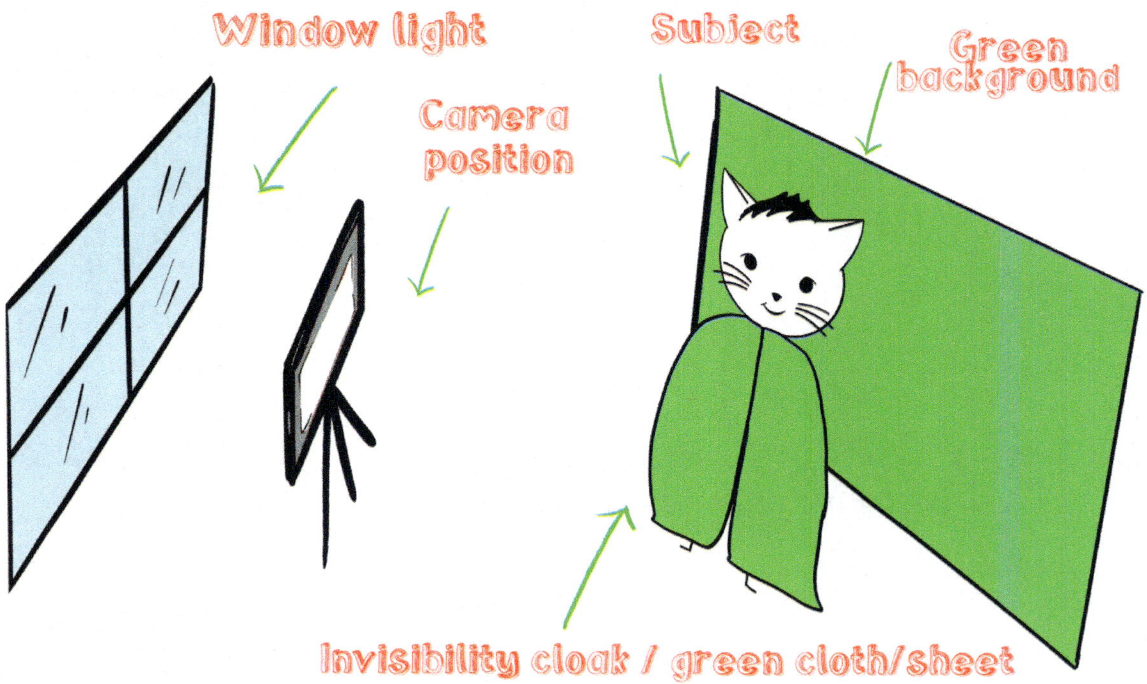

Once you record your actions or story you can get to work with adding an image over your green areas in the editing process. Go to the **'Editing with green screen video'** section in **Chapter 5** where Ted will show you how to edit your green screen.

TIPS AND TRICKS:

- You will need green fabric, pegs and some **HELP**. Ask your family to get involved in setting up as it can take more than one person to set up green screens properly.
- If you **make your own green screen background** make sure you keep your screen as flat as possible, so smooth out any creases or folds in the green fabric.
- Try to make sure the green screen is evenly lit for best image replacing results.

Have fun experimenting with what you can do!

Charlie

Thanks, Cherrybelle. That was super informative. I can't wait to see how the video turns out.

We've covered so much on **video making**, so let's draw up a list of **the things we might need to prepare to help make videos.** Marvela has designed the checklist in the backstage area. **CHECK IT OUT.**

Don't worry, you **don't need everything** on the list. Tick the things you might need for your next video creation.

See the backstage area (Chapter 8) for your full video preparation checklist.

Cherrybelle

Charlie, why don't you give them an example of how easy it is to make one of your YouTube videos **IRL**, using the **video plan**? How about creating a video about 'making pizza' for your new channel?

Charlie

Yes, **brilliant idea.** What better way to explain than to **show and tell** a real life example? Although I'm not sure about **pizza** anymore. I was thinking about doing a **history** channel from a cat's perspective. **Or** there's always my **lifestyle videos**. I've always wanted a lifestyle channel but **style** isn't my strongest point; I only own one T-shirt, one hoodie and a set of PJs!

Cherrybelle

How about we just stick to pizza because I know you love pizza and you're always giving your pizza making and ordering tips away when we come around to yours.

Charlie

You're right, Cherrybelle. Let's do it! Thanks for keeping me focussed BTW. I do love pizza and I shall share how to make my **special super food pizza**.

MAKING A VIDEO WITH CHARLIE

Marvela

Charlie, what's your video about?

Charlie

It's about pizza.

Marvela

And more specifically?

Charlie

It's all about how to make a vegetarian pizza with tuna.

Marvela

Ahem. No offence, Charlie, but you might want to double check what vegetarian means.

Okay, let's start by **creating my video plan.** I need to:

- ○ Design my **story board**
- ○ Write my **script**
- ○ Check what **video equipment** I need

Creating my video plan, storyboard & script

I am going to outline the **beginning, middle and end** of my video and include an outline of my **intro** and **outro**.

Beginning of video:

Video style: Live action – me talking direct to camera.

Scene location: Kitchen table.

Scene description: I will introduce myself and tell the viewer what the video is about. I will explain that I am going to make a very special pizza with a secret sauce that I will reveal to them.

Intro scene and script:

Script 1: Hello, my feline friends. Welcome to my channel, where I make all kinds of pizza. If you're new here, then thank you for joining me.

Beginning scene and script:

Script 2: In this video I'm going to show you how to make a very special vegetarian pizza. But this isn't any old pizza, this is my homemade super food pizza, with my very own special secret sauce which I will reveal exclusively to you, **my feline community**.

Script 3: To make this pizza you will need the following ingredients...(show and list all ingredients needed).

Middle of video:

Video style: Live action – film ingredients and food shots only.

Scene location: Kitchen table.

Scene descriptions: Show how to:

- Scene 1 - Make the dough
- Scene 2 - Make the secret sauce
- Scene 3 - Prepare the vegetables and toppings
- Scene 4 - Put all the layers together

Middle scenes and script:

Scene Script 1: You're in for a special treat. I want to make this very easy for you, so I am going to split out what you need to do into 3 easy parts.

I will describe **how to make the dough.**

Scene Script 2: I will describe how to make the secret sauce and mention how many generations this secret sauce has been passed down through my favourite pizza restaurants.

Scene Script 3: I will talk through the reasons I have chosen the toppings. Cheese for the tangy taste, peppers for crunch and colour, and spinach for superpowers. I will suggest other toppings viewers can use.

Scene Script 4: I will show the pizza ready to go into the oven. I will tell the viewers how long the pizza needs to go into the oven for, with the specific cooking instructions to get a delightful, delicious pizza base.

I will also highlight any safety precautions and suggest getting an adult to help with the oven, temperature and timings for those that cannot reach or read the oven knobs.

I will mention tips and the clearing up.

End of video:

Video style: Live action – me talking direct to camera.

Scene location: Kitchen table.

Scene description: Show the final results – the cooked pizza.

End scene and script:

Script 1: I take a bite out of the pizza and express how super delicious it is. I will remind everyone how super this pizza is, rich in lots of super foods to make them smarter than they already are and make them realise that Margherita and Pepperoni are so last century. (Personally, they'll always be my favourite no matter what century we're in!)

Outro and script:

Script 1: Thank you for watching and I hope you enjoyed it.

Script 2: If you want to see me making pizza with my grandma, where she shows me exactly how to make her secret special dough balls recipe, then check out my YouTube channel for more videos coming up on that. See you next time.

That's it. Well done!

Now that you've got the **video planned out**, let's start filming.

Ted

Charlie, is it necessary to create a video plan?

Charlie

Hey Ted, thanks for joining us and great question. You can make a video without a plan but it's much easier to make a really interesting or entertaining video **with a plan.** Many **YouTube creators** use a plan but they may not have started that way.

Ted

I see. Well, I'm not sure if I want to bother with all that. Seems like a lot of trouble. I just want to get straight to the filming.

Charlie

Sure, I hear ya, Ted. You can go ahead, hit the record button and make a fairly decent video. The best way is to do it your way, see what works for you, and what feels easy and comfortable. However, if you're hoping to make lots of videos over time then a **video plan may help you stay organised, get things done**, make great videos, and allow you **more time to spend on creating new ideas** for new videos.

If you're like Ted and don't want to bother with creating a video plan, you're in luck as **I've made a done-for-YOU video planner guide.** Just print or copy it out and use it for each video you want to make. **HAVE A GO** and see if it works for you.

Marvela has created some fantastic checklists for you too. All you need to do is check and tick...it couldn't be easier!

See the backstage area (Chapter 8) for your video planner guide and checklists.

TIPS AND TRICKS:

Get your family involved when planning your video. They can come up with some helpful ideas and may even volunteer to assist you during the making of your videos. They may be able to contribute or inspire you to come up with some great ideas for your video. Get them involved by **discussing and writing your video plan together**.

Batch filming: Try planning to film several videos in one go. As you have gone to the effort of setting up your film set, it makes it worthwhile to try and record a couple of videos, or more, in one go.

- **STEP 1.** Plan a day you want to create your videos and decide how many videos you want to make.
- **STEP 2.** Write down what each video is about.
- **STEP 3.** Make a list of the equipment, props and lighting you will need for each video and get them ready.
- **STEP 4**. Get filming!

You can **edit your videos** at the same time at a later stage, but getting the recording done in one go is very helpful. Put the video details in your video planner!

HAVE A GO: SKETCH A VIDEO STORYBOARD.

See the backstage area (Chapter 8) for your video planner, storyboard and scripts. You can copy, print and photocopy these as many times as you like in order to sketch out your many brilliant video ideas.

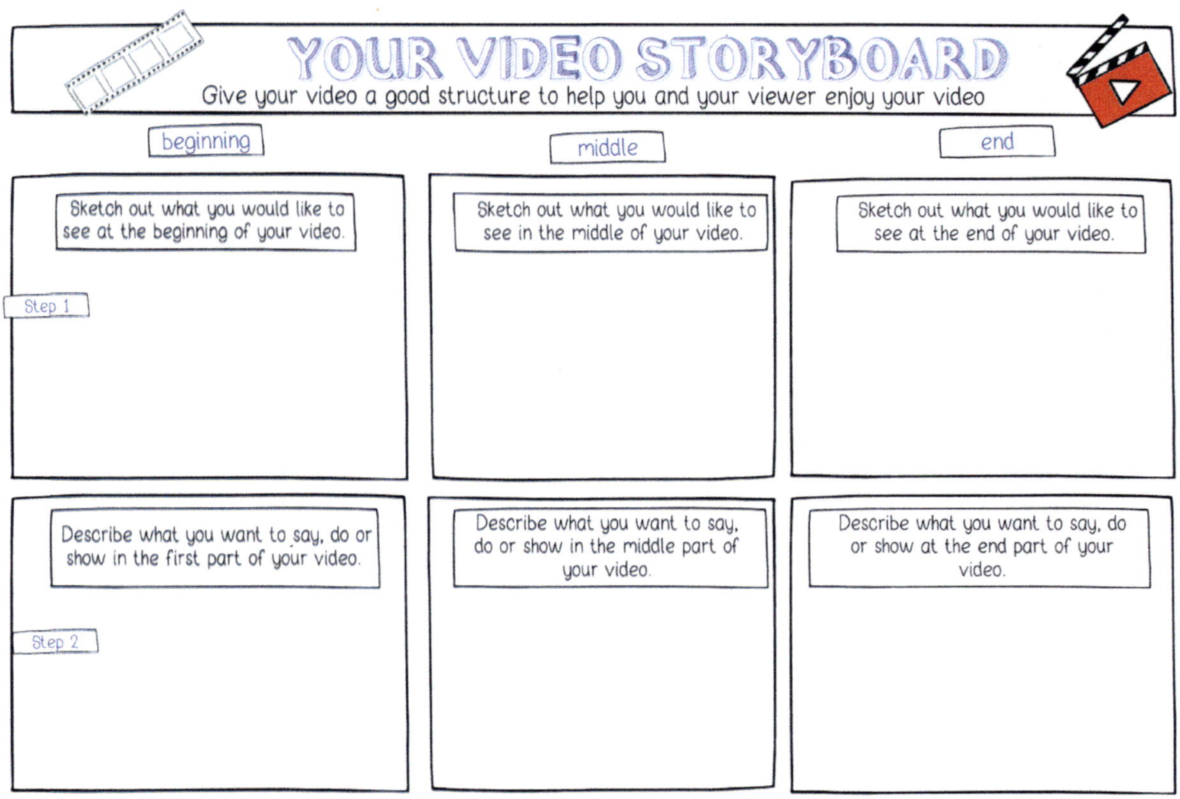

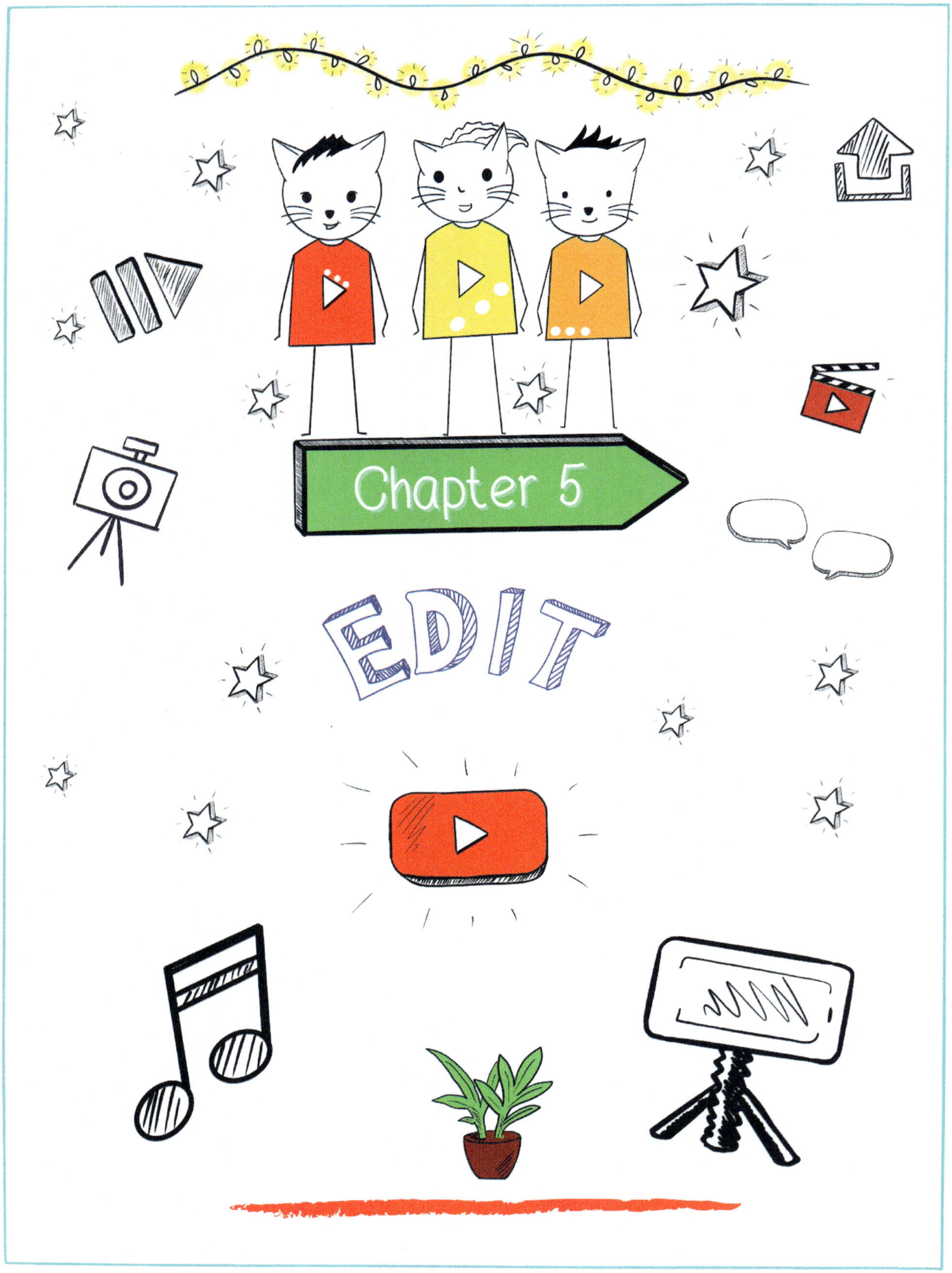
Chapter 5
EDIT

CHAPTER 5: EDIT

HOW TO EDIT YOUR VIDEOS LIKE A PRO

By now you **know how to record and film your videos – yay**! Well done! I bet you're super eager to know how to easily put everything together using video effects, transitions and music, and then upload them to **YouTube** for the world to see (well, at least for your friends and family to see for now).

Best editing apps to use

After you've finished filming the different parts or scenes of your video, you are ready to **'stick' it together** in the process known as **EDITING**. Once edited, your video is complete and ready to upload to **YouTube** and **share with** what I call the **FFFs** – your family, friends and fans.

You can **make your video stand out** and create a fun experience for your viewers if you give your video a little **RAZZLE DAZZLE** or **THE WOW FACTOR**. For this you will need help from my **SPECIAL EFFECTS GURU** (not a real **guru** or **saint**...but close!) and **EDITING EXTRAORDINAIRE – TED**. He popped in a little earlier. Personally, **I love editing**, it's my favourite bit. Check out his Bio.

Ted's a total **whizz at graphic design** and the master at editing. He taught me everything I know. **Thank you, Ted!** He can literally take me anywhere in the world with a little **green screen wizardry** and he's got enough photoshop magic to make **Harry Potter** green (screen) with envy. I absolutely **LOVE** Ted! Don't get me wrong, I do my own editing (that's what most of us YouTubers do for the most part) but Ted certainly taught me a thing or two. Now he's here to give you a bunch of special tips to make it quick and easy for you to grasp the editing process too.

Once, he taught me how to land on the moon, swim with a swarm of stingrays, and enter into my pet hamster's cage. My favourite experience was when he showed me how I could perform my favourite song on a virtual stage in front of thousands of peeps just like you! Of course, there was quite a bit of trickery involved.

So, without further ado, here's Ted.

Bio

NAME:

Ted

Specialist knowledge: Graphics, special effects and editing

Good points: Has constantly great ideas and makes videos look and sound fandabidozee (that's a good thing BTW!)

Loves: Video games and chemistry

Favourite YouTube Topics: Camera equipment, basketball, gardening and smoothie recipes

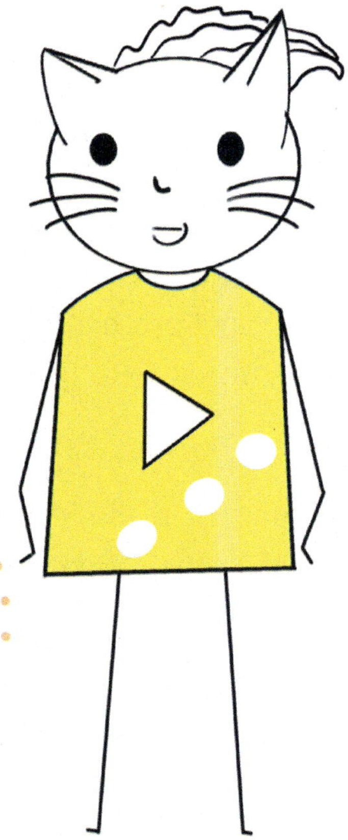

Ted

Thanks for the awesome intro, Charlie. I didn't know you felt that way about me. Chuffed. Nice to e-meet you and virtual greetings from behind my editing suite.

Charlie

Ted, tell us what video editing is and why we need it for video making.

Ted

Using your pizza analogy, the editing stage of video making forms part of the third layer on the pizza – the toppings. Editing helps make your video complete by making sure it's exactly how you want it to look and sound (or, in the case of a pizza, how it tastes) so that it's ready to consume (I mean watch). It's like putting the final polish to your creation.

These days there are so many ways you can 'glue' all your great video clips together and make other edits. You don't need fancy or expensive editing software, for now you can just use the software that comes with your laptop or device, for example, Apple devices come with iMovie.

There are so many good editing apps you can use on tablets and mobiles. For example, CapCut is a very popular one, and there's also InShot, Adobe Premiere Rush, CutStory, Clips, KineMaster, Canva and Funimate. There's even YouTube's own called YouTube Create. These are great for gaining some quick editing skills and they're perfectly easy to use. Charlie mentioned some of these earlier in the book, but whichever editing app(s) you choose to use **REMEMBER** to get permission before downloading and installing them.

REMEMBER to ask for permission and supervision from a parent / guardian before downloading apps.

Editing is fun and I believe it's where the **VIDEO MAGIC** begins. You can literally make **things appear and disappear**! And you can add **SPECIAL EFFECTS**. They're not called 'special effects' for no reason you know – they're pretty special and very effective.

Editing forms part of the **post-production** part of the video making process. It's the time and place where you organise all the video clips you have filmed and recorded.

Glossary: Post-production editing is the process of putting your video together and all the extra work done once it has been filmed and recorded, like adding all the video clips together, adding special effects, transitions, filters and music.

Charlie

But how do you edit the video clips together? Can you explain how it works?

Of course. All you have to do is place your **video clip files on to a timeline** in your editing app. Your timeline looks like a very long horizontal strip. Your video clips can come in a number of **different file formats**, and usually end with a file name such as **.MP4** or **.Mov.**

So, let's use the example of Charlie's pizza making video.

If we were to edit this video, we would need to gather all the video clips Charlie recorded.

We would import these video clips into our editing software and place each video clip or scene on the timeline in the order we want them to go. We can look at the video planner to double check what order the scenes should be in. If we follow the video planner and storyboard, it's easy to create the video we set out to make.

Ted

We then need to drag the correct file clips or scene into the timeline. Once all the correct film clips are placed next to each other (again, in the right order), we can decide to use clever ways to make it one finished video. Basically, we want to stick the recorded clips together and we often use special effects or transitions for this.

Cherrybelle

It's like putting a puzzle together.

Charlie

You're right, you need to know in which order the video clips or scenes need to go. It's easy to get in a muddle here, but the planner works to help keep things simple and on track.

Cherrybelle

What's a jump cut? I hear this term a lot from the editing guys. And what's a transition?

Ted

Good questions. Let me come on to those now...

Transitions

Transitions are the cool slides that you add to make **one scene / clip flow seamlessly into another scene / clip**. They can be gradual or impactful but they are always interesting. You can have transitions, such as **fades**, **directional slide-ins** or **blurs**.

You don't always need transitions but they help make a video look smooth, seamless or impactful. Transitions help add some polish to your final video. You can become a pretty **Slick Mick** when you do this.

Jump cuts appear much sharper and quicker and tend to go from one scene / clip to another without a transition. You'll see a lot of these in YouTube videos, and it's very easy and effective to create, mainly because you don't have to add any transitions. You just put your recorded clips side by side in the right order. It's just lots of **WYSIWYG pronounced 'whizzy wig'** – What You See Is What You Get.

How to add transitions:

Find the transitions in your preferred editing app.

Drag and drop your chosen transition in between the 2 film clips that you want to 'stick' or edit together.

If you don't use transitions your scenes may look a bit **JUMPY** when they go from one to another. It's quite common to see these in YouTube videos, however, it's great fun to have a go at seeing which transitions work for you and your specific video.

TIPS AND TRICKS:

- There are many cool transitions so it's worth taking some time to get to know your app and checking through them all and experimenting.
- Always pick the one that you feel works well with your story or video topic. For example, if you're in your garden talking about sea pollution and then want to cut to a shot of the beach, you might want to use 'water ripples' as a transition style.
- There are so many transitions to choose from so try a few out and select what works for you.

Cut and trim

When editing, **focus on using your best video clips**, or the scenes that clearly tell a story / give a message / show how to make pizza / show the best gameplay. It's unlikely that you'll use all the clips you've filmed or animated. You can easily remove or erase clips from your timeline that you don't want by using the **cut tool**. You can also trim down a scene. For example, you may have a perfect clip but you need to cut the first and last few seconds. In that case, all you need to do is click on the video clip and drag each end of the clip to the desired place.

Time lapse

Time lapse **speeds up your film**. It's perfect for those videos that show something being **created over a long period of time**, like art or cooking. You can film yourself painting, cooking or building a floating island in Minecraft. Speed up the middle section of the film so you can get to the finished result quickly.

Slow motion

Slow motion **slows down the action in your film**. This is one of my personal favourites and can add a nice interest point in your video. However, you don't want to do your whole video in slow motion. You can either add a slow motion effect in post production (editing stage) or you can set your video to a slow motion feature when filming live action.

Text effects

You can **add text onto your video** during the editing process too. Adding words onto your video is sometimes referred to as **text overlay**.

Adding text is a great way to make your message clearer. For example, you can **add text to outline the key words or messages you want to emphasise**, such as **'Thank you'** or **'Feed me pizza'** or anything **random**. It's completely up to you which words you use. You may want to use words to be funny or create impact but text overlay is a fun way to make your videos different. You can also **change the design of text** using fonts, colours and sizing, which usually comes as a feature of your editing app.

CLICK BOOM! WAY TO GO!

Another idea is to add text between scenes. For example, you could have the words **'Preparing the kitchen for pizza making'** followed by the making of pizza in the kitchen live action scene. Later on in your video, **the text 'After 15 minutes in the oven'** could appear on a plain background and then show the next scene of the pizza cooked and ready to serve.

You can also have text **fading** in or out, or **sliding** in or out, of your video. Whatever you do with text, adding it to your video is simple and it can certainly help make your video more impressive and fun to watch, as well as add a dramatic effect.

Charlie

How awesome is that? So how do we add text?

Ted

Easy! Just add another layer to your editing timeline and look for the text feature icon in your editing app. It usually looks like a capital T in a box.

You can usually find ready-made titles and text options in your editing app. Just click and drag them onto the part of the film timeline you want to add text to as another layer. As you get used to this feature, you can start to explore how to change the colour, font and sizing.

Adding images

You can **add photos, images and overlay video clips on to your video** too. It works in the same way as **text**. First, find an image you want to add, for example, a photo of the perfect pizza. Next, drag it to another layer in your editing timeline and place it on top of the scene where you want it to go. Then trim it to the length you want it to be and, voilà, you're done. Some YouTube game play videos resize their selfie commentary videos and make them smaller. This way they can overlay the small selfie video onto their main game play video. That is how the viewer can see the game play and the YouTuber at the same time.

Cherrybelle

What about filters, Ted. Do we need them?

Ted

FILTERS ARE FAB! Video filters can enhance the colouring of your film and make your video **POP**, or set a mood for the atmosphere you want to portray in your video.

Filters

You can add filters or adjust the colouring of your video easily these days. You can find filter features on most editing apps. For example, if you have a film clip of yourself talking to the camera and it's a bit of a dull or cloudy day, you can add a **'sunny' or 'bright' filter**. Usually, it's a case of dragging and dropping your chosen filter effect over your film strip in your **editing timeline**, then your video will instantly go from a **dull to a brighter image**. This is a particularly good trick if your video clip was filmed in low light.

Some filters allow you to **add different styles to your film clips**. For example, you can **make an ordinary film look like an animated cartoon** or add a **cinematographic style** to make your video look like a Hollywood or Bollywood movie. Black and white filters allow you to turn your video or part of your video into black and white which can give your video added **DRAMA** or **INTEREST**. Different editing apps have different in-built filters available but there will always be something that adds to your video.

TIPS AND TRICKS:

- The main point to bear in mind is that adding filters **enhances** your video and creates the right **mood**.
- My tip is to stay as close to natural as possible unless you're doing an experimental abstract video piece. In which case, GO CRAZY CATS!

ADDING SPECIAL EFFECTS

Creating **SPECIAL EFFECTS** has to be my **NUMBER ONE FAVOURITE** thing to do...

There are so many ways you can **jazz up your video** with effects. It makes it more fun to watch, but nothing makes it more fun than adding the **odd crazy special effect** or two. **Check what special effects are available in your editing software**.

My favourite effects at the moment are the **smoky effect** which I add to create a **spooky atmosphere**. I also love the **cartoon** effect. That one is so **awesome** – it literally converts your film into animation! For example, Charlie would look **SUPER COOL** with an **animation EFFECT on his videos**, what do you think?.

Charlie

WAIT, WHAT?

If you know you want to add special effects **IRL** or during the filming process, then **make a note of this in your video plan** so you can record your videos with specific effects in mind. For example, you can use a garden sprinkler as pretend rain, or you can have one of your friends or family blow bubbles into the air during a scene to get a dreamy effect, or use an automatic bubble making machine (one of my personal favourite props – I have 3!). For these scenes you will need plenty of space when recording and ideally you will be outdoors.

BTW water and electronics is a **no no**. Make sure your camera or device is not going to get wet with bubble splashes, water or liquids.

Adding special effects during editing

Another example is if you wanted to **create a magic potion scene** in your video. Instead of creating the effects of the potion **IRL**, you can **add them on after** filming, in the editing stage.

All you need to do is record the action clip. This could be a film of your character holding a jar of coloured liquid and placing it onto a table surface. Pop the video clip into your editing timeline and **drag and drop your chosen smoke effect** onto it.

For example, to add a **puff of smoke** to the jar in the film clip, you need to:

- Find the special effect 'smoke' in your editing app
- Add it to the layer above your video timeline
- Place it on the scene you want it to appear in (for the duration you want)

Once it's complete your video will appear as if you have smoke coming out of a jar.

It's important to remember that although this seems like a fairly simple idea, creating **these effects in the editing process can get a little tricky at times**. So please don't try doing this by yourself if you're just starting out. Always get a parent or guardian involved to help you understand and use your editing app. Having said that, if you start editing with simple apps and keep learning and progressing, you will become a brilliant editor someday – I'm certain of that. It may even become a full time career when you're older!

TIPS AND TRICKS:

- For those of you out there that want to make your videos look like your favourite movie, listen up. **Check out all the effects and filters on your editing app** before you begin to edit your videos. See what you have available to use.
- Keep experimenting with your editing features so you become familiar with them. **Think about the mood you want to create** and the **effects you want to use** to make your videos the best they can be.

Cherrybelle

In Chapter 4, I was telling our budding YouTube creators about creating a fun **invisibility cloak** for a video using **green screen**. Can you explain how they can edit the video to get the final invisible effect?

Ted

That's a great idea! Of course, I will do that now. **I love making things disappear** in the editing process.

EDITING WITH GREEN SCREEN

You may hear **green screen** being referred to as **'chroma key'** but it means pretty much the same thing. All it means is that **you can replace any part of your video clip or film that has the green screen, with another image or colour**. Anything on your video clip that does not have green, will remain. So, if you had a green background then that can be replaced.

When you edit with green screen video, you need to add the **keying feature** onto your video clip. This process makes the green part of your video clip **fully transparent** so that another image of your choice can easily appear.

Glossary: Keying. This term is used to describe the green screen removal process in video editing apps and software.

Marvela

Does your backdrop or background have to be green?

Ted

That's a good question. In the old days they used to use blue, but nowadays green screen is more widely used. You can actually use any colour, however, **GREEN** is the colour that is furthest away from human skin tones and creates the most convincing effect. A lot of big movies use green screen in their scenes.

Random Fact Alert

Robert Rodriguez is a GREEN SCREEN movie making master. The actors in his film series 'Spy Kids' were filmed in front of green screens. In 'Spy Kids 3-D' gaming images were then placed over the green areas during editing stage which helped create the desired gaming world effect.

This is why when **you have a green cloak on and you stand in front of a green screen background**, you can swap out the green colour for something else. It can get a bit complicated so let's go through the basic principles using the invisibility cloak video Cherrybelle and Charlie made earlier.

- In the **invisibility cloak** video clip Charlie moves from one side of the screen to the other.
- He found the **keying effect** in the editing app **effects library in his editing software**.
- He dragged and dropped the keying effect onto the video clip (with the green screen).

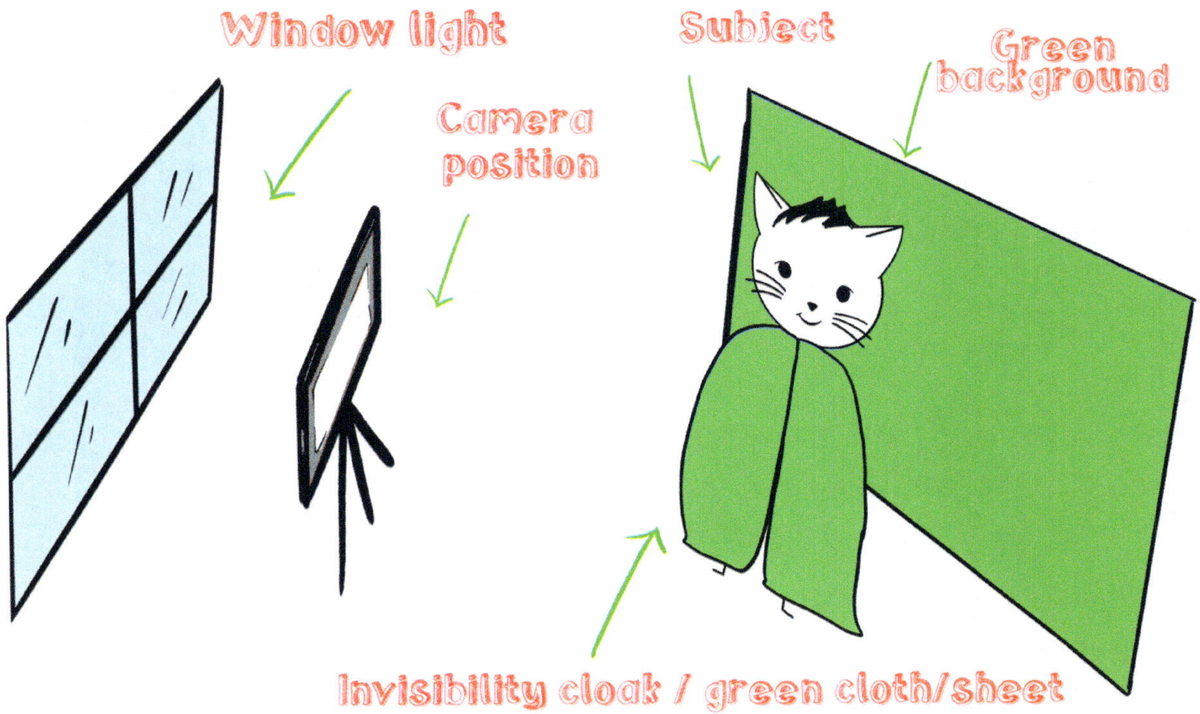

Let's explain further using Charlie's green screen video.

You should be able to see the video you are working on in your **editing viewer**.

In this case, Charlie is in the foreground wearing a green cloak and is standing in front of a green backdrop (background).

- Let's **add our chosen image of a creepy castle** above the green screen video clip in the edit suite timeline.
- Let's find the **keying effect** in the editing app effects library.
- Drag the **keying effect** onto the main green screen video clip of Charlie in his cloak (not the clip above but actually onto it).

And that's it. Once done, all you will see is Charlie's head bopping around a creepy castle. It's like **MAGIC**. The **keying feature removed everything green on**

Charlie's video clip apart from his head and replaced it with an image of a creepy castle.

Nice work! **THAT'S SO FREAKY BUT SOOOOOO AWESOME!** That's just given me a great idea for a **HALLOWE'EN** video I want to make!

When you are happy with your final video, export it and give it a name that describes the video so you can easily find and identify it. Then add it to your 'finished videos' folder until you're ready to upload.

Have fun exploring all the effects available in your editing app. You don't need to use too many effects to give your video a little polish. It can take years to perfect your editing skills so take your time and enjoy the process.

P.S. Less is more. ;)

TIPS AND TRICKS:

- If you are using green screen, remember **not to wear green** or have lots of green objects in your video unless you want them to disappear!

- If you can't find the keying feature in your editing app it probably doesn't have one available. Not all editing apps come with green screen or keying features.
- Green screen editing can get a bit complicated but if you're a curious cat and want to know more then get help from a parent, guardian or teacher. They can help find the right editing app and have fun with editing too.
- **HAVE A GO** at making a green screen video at home, have a play around with the editing, and keep practising! Practice makes perfect.
- Always remember to export and save your edited work.
- Get help with your editing when you're just starting out and practise editing with test videos before you make your special videos.
- Be aware that all the different elements – text, film clips, audio etc. – sit on different layers in your editing timeline. They flatten or merge together to form your final creation when you export your final video.
- You can add your gaming film clips to your editing timelines. You can cut bits out, add a voice over and even add your face cam film clips if you have them. You need to shrink your face cam clips to a thumbnail size and place over the main gaming film layer.

CHECK OUT THE EDITING TIMELINE ILLUSTRATIONS BELOW TO GET AN IDEA OF WHAT TO EXPECT. Each layer in the timeline needs to be in the right layering order depending on what you want to see in the foreground of your video. (The illustrations below will give you some idea of what you can expect to see in your editing software or apps).

Editing timelines

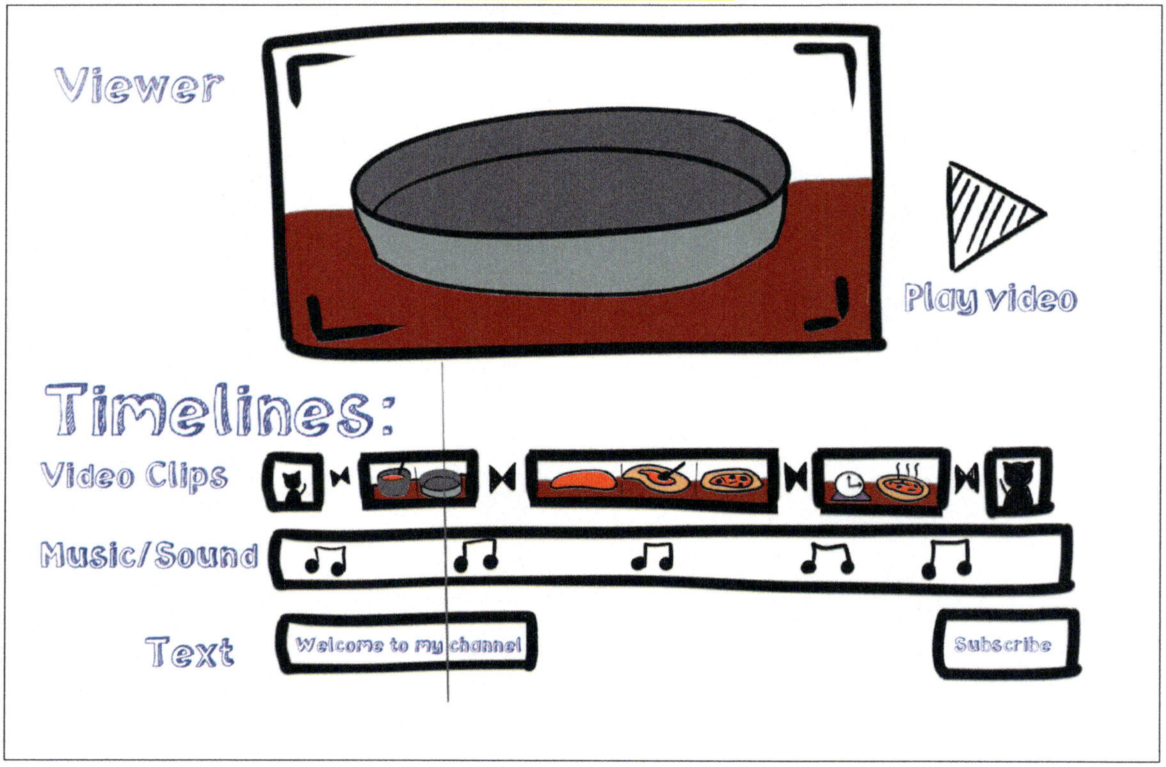

Editing timeline with green screen

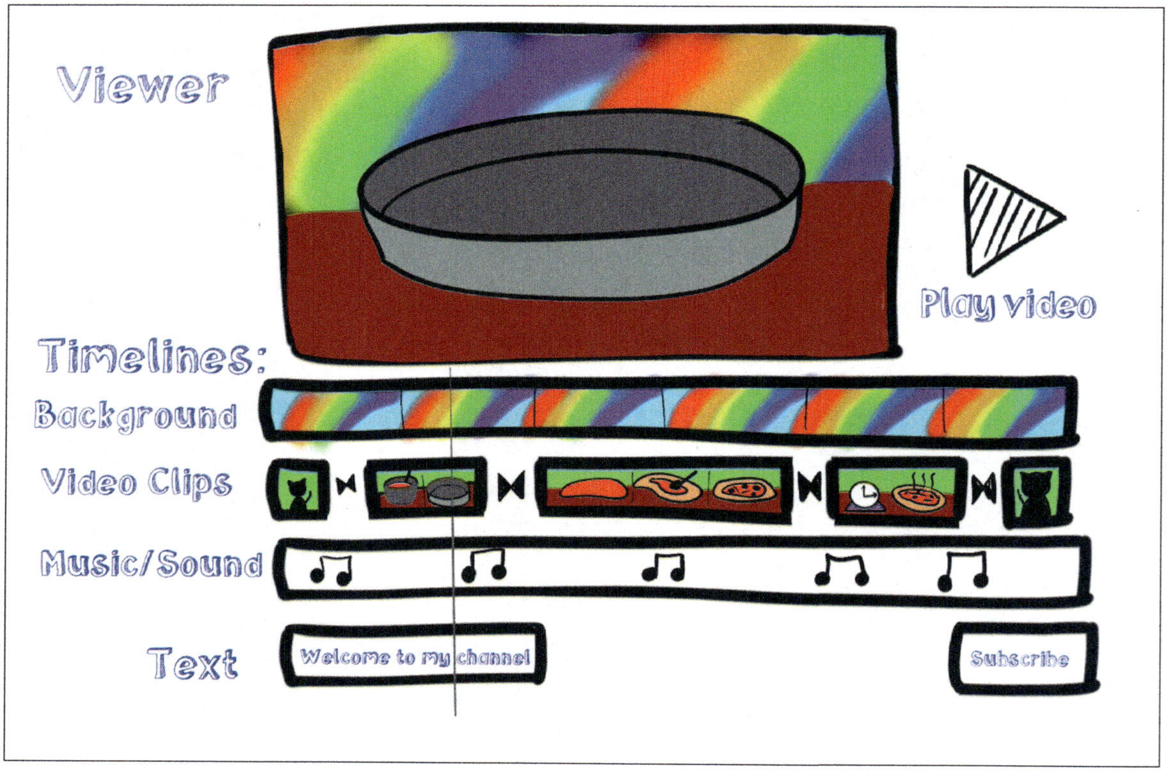

Editing timeline for a gaming video with face cam

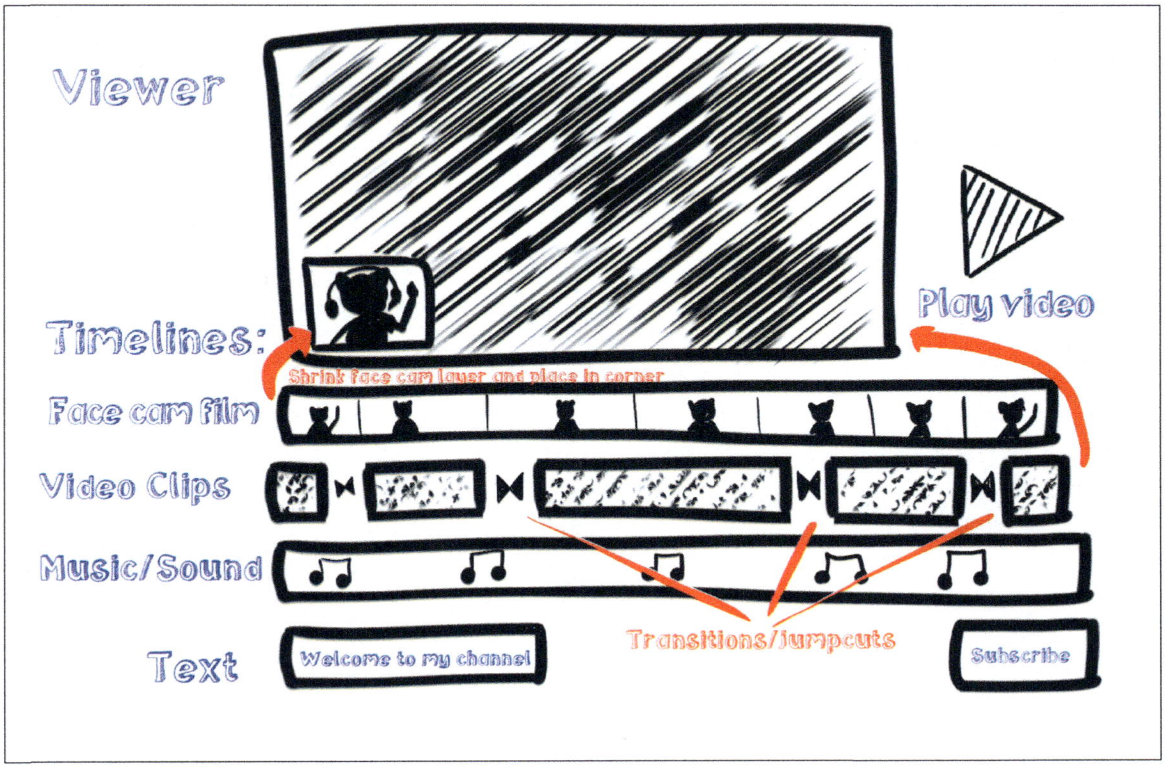

Q&A

Cherrybelle

What are the best editing apps I can use?

Ted

If you want a quick edit or you're just starting out, I recommend using one of the many editing apps out there. I've given some recommendations in Chapter 8 so check that out. You can use these on most **tablets** and **smartphones**.

Ted

There's even **apps that can make cool intros and outros** which you can add to your video.

Then, as you become a bit older and more of a pro, you can go on to use something more advanced Adobe Premier Pro, DaVinci Resolve or Final Cut Pro. The list of good options is endless, but I recommend starting with the free or inexpensive simple apps.

RANDOM FACT ALERT

The first tablets date back to the BRONZE Age and into the IRON Age (about 3000 years ago). They were used by SCRIBES for communication and recording events. A pen made out of REED was impressed onto a WET CLAY TABLET and left to harden. A bit like today, these tablets came in a variety of colours, bone white, chocolate, and charcoal.

Cherrybelle

What about music and sound effects? How do I add those to my video?

Ted

These are pretty easy to add, and you can have a lot of fun with them.

Music and sound effects

I love **SOUND EFFECTS** – they make my videos feel really authentic and they are **soooo much fun** to play around with. You can find almost any sound you like, for example, a clock ticking, a creaky door, a door slamming shut, birds chirping, a dog barking or footsteps. (**I do my own meowing BTW** – being so **AUTHENTIC** it sets me apart from other **cool cats**!)

You can add sounds to your videos that might add to the overall theme. For example, if you're doing a Hallowe'en video you might want to add some spooky sounds like creaky doors, spooky music or footsteps.

TIPS AND TRICKS:

- Make sure your sound (also referred to as audio) is not too loud. You can keep the **sound levels** steady so they are easy for the viewer to enjoy.
- You can **download sound effects from various places**, but YouTube has a library and you can use lots of sounds for free.
- Get your parent(s) or guardian(s) to help out and find stuff with you. It can take a lot of time but it's a **lotta, lotta fun**!

AHHHHH snare drum roll please – **it's the BIG ONE**...

THE EASY WAY!

THE MUSIC!

Charlie

It's time to introduce my **MUSO** friend, Sam. Hey bro, can you tell us a little about your experience with **MUSIC AND VIDEO**?

Bio

NAME:

Sammy

Specialist knowledge: Creator studio back end

Good points: Whizz kid at making YouTube channels grow with his magnificent magic powers and metadata skills

Loves: Music making, gaming and storyboarding

Favourite YouTube Topics: Music, Minecraft, Game Theory and history

Sam

Sure thing. BTW would you like me to talk about how to **upload video** too?

Charlie

Yes please, tell us about that in Chapter 6 when we start to upload our video. For now, tell us about your experience with **MUSIC** and **YouTube**?

Sam

From my personal experience, when I started my first YouTube channel, I made my own music and added it to my videos. Even though a lot of my music was based on songs written by people hundreds of years ago, I received a lot of **copyright strike notifications**. I found it confusing to understand whether I could use my own songs that I had recorded at home.

Charlie

Can I use other people's music in my videos or will I get a copyright strike?

Sam

If you get permission from the owner of the music and credit them in your video then using their music is allowed (depending on the license). This isn't something I imagine you would need to get involved in as you start out, but it's always good to know what to look out for in the future.

Glossary: Copyright. When someone creates a piece of work they own the work and it is protected by copyright. This means no one else can use it without permission.

Over the years, YouTube have improved their technology and now you can add **royalty free music to your videos**, so you don't need to worry about all of that copyright business.

Glossary: Royalty free is unowned music and sound that is available for anyone to use for free.

Charlie

HIP HOP HURRAY, the YouTube music library sounds **AMAZING!**

One great **YouTube** resource that I've seen grow over the years is the creation of **YouTube's GINORMOUS music library.** I've seen their music library grow with new sound and music being added all the time. It's a **huge help for all creators**, especially for those like you who are just starting out and don't need to bother too much with getting music permissions and all that **JAZZ**.

Glossary: Copyright strike is when Person A uses music written, created and owned by Person B. Person B protects their work with a copyright and can ask YouTube to remove Person A's video if they haven't asked and received permission to use it. YouTube then removes Person A's video to comply with copyright law.

The music library contains a very long list of music of all genres and it also contains a whole bunch of **sounds effects** that you can download and use on your videos for **free**. You won't get any copyright strikes if you stick to using music and sound from YouTube's library. In some cases, however, you may need to credit the song or music writer in your video description. It will tell you clearly if you need to.

YouTube's library of music and sound effects have been selected so that you will probably find something that works with your video topic.

You can choose different styles of music, from hip hop to classical, and you can also choose different sounds.

Charlie

Where can I find YouTube's music library?

Sam

- Go to your YouTube creator studio
- Head over to the left side column
- Scroll down towards the bottom and look for **YouTube library**. That's where it was the last time I checked.

You can search for the style of music or sounds and listen to previews. If you like, you can download the music or sound file when you're done. These are digital files and usually end with **.MP3.**

The music library is so comprehensive that you may be in **DANGER** of spending more time in the **YouTube library** than your own local library!

Ted

That's **EPIC**! Thanks, Sam. Can I just add something?

Sam

Sure. Be my guest...

Ted

Sorry, I don't mean add to what you're sayng, I mean can I just **ADD ANY** music or sounds to my video?

Let me explain. Once you decide on your **music or sound effects**, add them to your **editing timeline**. Decide where you want to place the music, or where you want the sound effect(s) to appear in your video, then drag the music or sound **.MP3** file over where you want it to go. You should see the sound create a new layer on the timeline. You can easily click on the music layer if you want to move, trim or delete it.

TIPS AND TRICKS:

- Have a go at making and recording **your own sound effects**, and making your own music and sound library. For example, you can use a recording app to record **footsteps**, a door **slamming**, **laughter** or **clapping**. Get your family involved and see what sort of sounds you can all make together.
- Be careful to make sure your sound levels are even so that your sound is not too loud or too low when you play back the video.
- There are lots of other royalty free music and sounds resources but, for now, try the YouTube music library or create your own music, songs and sound.
- You can monetise your video content if you own it *100%*.
  Always make sure you have permission to use another artist's music. **Credit them in your description.**

Q&A

Marvela

What about cover songs? What happens if I want to sing my favourite song?

Sam

It seems that most music artists don't mind if you cover or use their songs and music. But I suggest you **always credit the original songwriter** in your description box. This is something that may affect your **monetisation** but I'm sure Charlie will cover that in his next book – hey Charlie?

Charlie

Wait. What?

Glossary: Monetise is the term YouTube uses for its official program that allows users to make money from the clips they upload. Monetisation most often applies to YouTube creator pros that become a YouTube partner. To become a YouTube partner and monetise your YouTube channel videos you need to have at least 4000 minutes watch time and have had 1000 subscribers in the last 12 months.

RANDOM FACT ALERT

The FIRST EVER VIDEO UPLOADED to YOUTUBE was of an elephant during a visit to the zoo filmed by the original YouTube creators! And while we're at it, DID YOU KNOW that elephants have the LARGETS BRAIN OF ANY LAND MAMMAL?

HAVE A GO:

RECORD OR FIND AUDIO CLIPS

See the backstage area (Chapter 8) for links to places where you can get free to use sound effects, music and images for your videos for post production and editing. You can also check out links to YouTube support and help for further information.

Chapter 6

UPLOAD

CHAPTER 6: UPLOAD

UPLOAD YOUR VIDEOS TO YOUTUBE

Now that you've **planned**, **recorded** and **edited** your video **AND** it's looking exactly how you imagined, you're ready for your **FFFs** (friends, family and fans) to see it. Let's set forth and upload it to your **YouTube channel and send them the link so that they can watch your AWESOME video**!

How to upload your videos:

You need to upload your video in the **YouTube studio of your YouTube channel account.**

1. **Click** the little round icon in the top right hand corner of your YouTube Channel. It looks like this:

Scroll down and click on **YouTube Studio**.

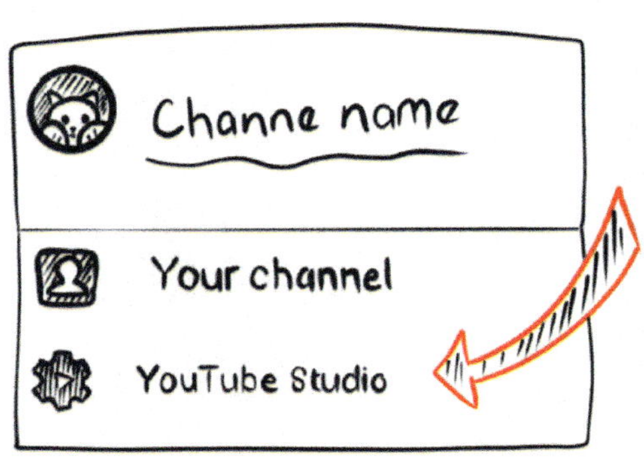

2. Stay in the top right hand corner of your account and you will see a camera icon with a **PLUS** sign which says **CREATE**. Click here and you will see 3 options. Click the first one which says '**Upload videos**'.

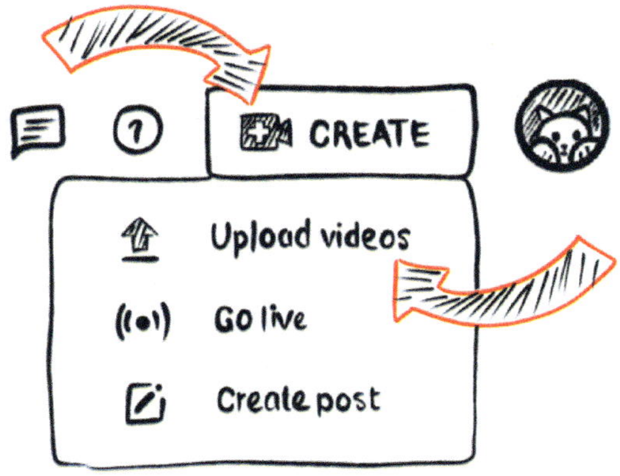

Or you can see the same icons in the top right hand corner under the red camera icon with the plus sign and your round channel icon.

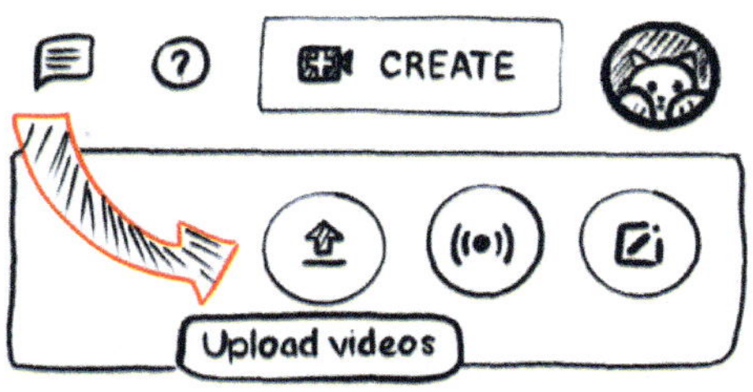

3. Add your finished video from wherever you saved your video file(s). You can **drag and drop** your finished **.MP4 or .MOV** video file directly from your finished video folder into the **YouTube upload page.**

4. You will see a number of different options to go through. Firstly, select '**Details**' on the left of the line below. Here you should add your video **title**, **description**, **tags** and **thumbnail**. (We'll talk more about these later in this chapter.)

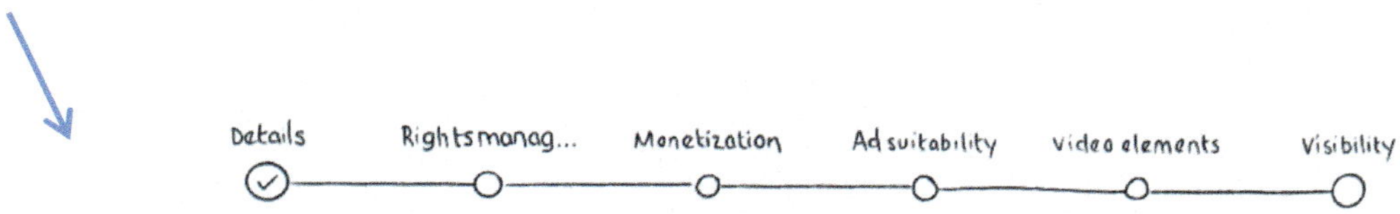

You need to go through each of the steps above every time you upload a video to **YouTube**. Go through these steps with a parent or guardian as it can get a little technical and confusing when you're just starting out. Perhaps you can hand them this chapter if they don't already know how to upload videos – it should help to get them started too and they will be able to check the all the right boxes have been ticked to meet **YouTube's** guidelines and online safety. (they can also check out the YouTube support links in Chapter 8)

See the backstage area (Chapter 8) for links to YouTube support, community guidelines, video training and lots more help.

When you upload your video, you can make it available to **watch immediately** or you can set it to be available to watch at a **particular time on a particular day**. This is the '**Schedule**' option. You can find it in the '**Visibility**' tab in the menu line.

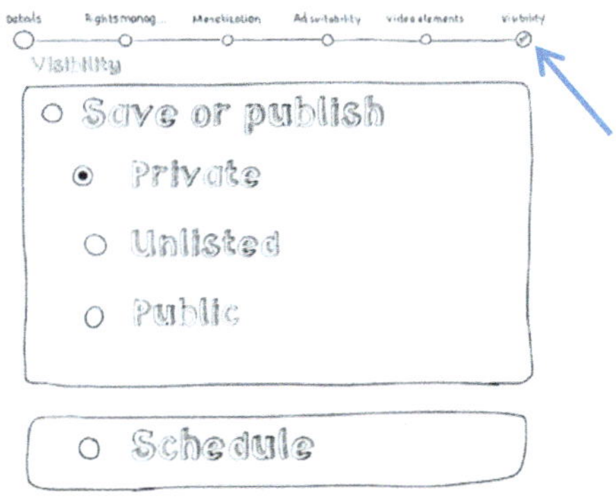

I find that **scheduling my videos** for a future time and date gives me time to show my YouTube video to my **nearest and dearest**. It allows me to make any suggested changes or improvements. I highly recommend this. If you need to make changes it's easy to remove the scheduled video and upload the newly changed version.

I've been uploading YouTube videos for **SOOOO long** that I can even do it in my sleep. As a **pro YouTuber** I hit the **autopilot upload switch in my brain** and away I go...**racking up those views at the speed of light** and entertaining my vast fanbase of 21 peeps. It's quality not quantity remember.

If you want to be an **awesome YouTuber** like your favourite creators, or you're at the beginning of your **YouTube journey**, you will continue to learn and develop your video skills. There's a lot to it but **REMEMBER** the **TRUE SECRET** is to practise, experiment and **ENJOY**.

Q&A

Sam

So, what's the best way to start creating a great YouTube channel?

Charlie

Well, to start with you need to:

- Make a video plan
- Keep making videos
- Export your well labelled video files to a video folder
- Stay organised!

Marvela

FANS-TASTIC! BTW I'm liking the list, Charlie! Well done - I'm proud of you!

Charlie

Thanks **Marvelous Marvela**! I'm a quick learner and have a **great teacher**.

Now that you have come so far in this book, and learnt the secrets to starting your **YouTube channel** and making **fans-tastic videos**, I think it's time to acknowledge your achievement. To do this I would like you to **say the following declaration out loud to yourself**:

"I (say your name) know what it takes to make awesome YOUTUBE videos and can easily get started on making my own YouTube channel"!

If you agree, you are officially **READY TO PROCEED**. (If you don't agree with the statement above then go back to page 1, re-read the first 5 chapters, and then come back here and say the declaration out loud.)

YOU ARE READY TO CONTINUE TO THE NEXT ROUND!

TIPS AND TRICKS:

- Your video does not have to be available to everyone at the time you upload it. You can set your video to **PRIVATE** or **UNLISTED.** This means that for private videos **only you will be able to see** your video and for **unlisted videos only you and those you share your video link with can see it**.
- For example, you can upload a video today and it will stay **PRIVATE** until a particular **date and time in the future that you want to make it PUBLIC** and share it with everyone. This is called a **SCHEDULED video.**
- You can also set it to **UNLISTED** and only the people you send the link to, like your family and friends, can see your video. This is also a great way to start your **YouTube creator journey**. Share your YouTube unlisted video link with friends and family and see what they think of your video masterpieces.

HOW TO GET VIDEO VIEWS & SUBSCRIBERS

CONGRATULATIONS! Your video is uploaded and published so people can watch it. **YAY!** Now that you've got to this point, you're probably thinking you can sit back and let YouTube bring in those views.

Alas, it doesn't work that way! There is still a little more work to do. If you want to be a pro, then it requires more work than just sharing your video link with your BFFs. The **good news** is that there is an **easy way** to reach more peeps so that they can watch and enjoy your video.

First of all, it's important to understand that **YouTube** isn't **PSYCHIC**. It cannot read your mind. It has no idea what your video is about and who might be interested in it, and therefore it doesn't know who to send it to. This is where your **clever brain** comes in as you need to help **YouTube's algorithm** show your videos to peeps who are looking for your video topics. Every minute, millions of video creators around the world **upload millions of videos** to YouTube. It's a big video universe.

(This is another reason why you need to make sure your parent(s) or guardian(s) supervise your video channel until you're old enough and ready to manage it yourself.)

The way to get your videos seen by the **right fans** is to make sure that you are super clever at **labelling your video when you upload**. You need to tell the YouTube algorithm to **notice your video and suggest it to peeps** who are looking for your video topic. This way it will be shown to more peeps who are likely to be fans. It's pretty magical but **it can't do it without your help**. You're probably wondering how you do this so I'm going to get some help. Come with me.

RANDOM FACT ALERT

ADA LOVELACE was the world's first computer programmer. She wrote the world's first machine algorithm entirely on paper, for an early computing machine. She was the daughter of Lord Byron, a POET, POLITICIAN, and leader of the ROMANTIC movement.

Glossary: Algorithm. According to YouTube, their algorithm is a coding system (or computer programme) that is able to show viewers videos that are relevant to their interests, topics and hobbies. It likes to find the right video for the right viewer at the right time.

Let me introduce Professor Alga Rhythm. The prof. will explain how it works in a much simpler way.

Charlie

Professor, would you like to explain how the **algorithm** works to help get videos discovered and found by fans?

Bio

NAME:
Prof. Alga Rhythm

Specialist knowledge: Artificial intelligence, biometrics, face and speech recognition, optimisation of anything
Good points: Very sociable, organised, quick learner,
Loves: Maths, physics, robots, coding and electronic dance music
Favourite YouTube Topics: Maths, Science, humane technology and animals

Prof. Alga Rhythm

Thank you, I will do my best to communicate that. I, Professor Alga Rhythm, watch millions of videos daily (with help from some very advanced technologies **AKA artificial intelligence** (AI), **machine learning** and some real humans – there are a lot of videos to check through!).

Glossary: Artificial intelligence (AI) refers to machines that are programmed to think and behave like humans by copying human actions. The term can be applied to machines that appear to act like the human mind in the way they learn and problem solve. Artificial intelligence (AI) is the refers to machines that are programmed to think and behave like humans by copying human actions. The term can be applied to machines that appear like the human mind, such as learning and problem-solving. It refers to all sorts of data points including voice activation and image recognition.

We watch every video to check **what the videos are about** so that we can be sure they are **suitable for viewers and that the video meets YouTube's guidelines.** If there are no problems they get to stay on YouTube, and we show the video to people we think will be interested in the video topic. The viewers may become fans or subscribers after watching it. If a video does not pass the test, or disobeys **YouTube's rules**, then we may block the video and notify the YouTube creator. It's not perfect yet but we're pretty close. We're still learning ourselves and always improving our processes to make it work better.

Glossary: YouTube's community guidelines are designed to protect the YouTube community. They outline what is and isn't allowed on YouTube. This includes video content, comments, links and thumbnails.

Here's the thing...it's not always easy for the team to show all videos to YouTube viewers because **we have to judge what's in the video**. Because we are machines and cannot see, like you cats or humans, we have to go on what you tell us in your video labelling and description.

We need to get some ideas about the video from you. We like **words and clear images**, which we sometimes refer to as **METADATA.**

Charlie

Thx Prof. So, basically, YouTube creators need to learn how to add these **clues and information to their video during the upload process** so you can **suggest** their video to the relevant kinds of fans who may be interested in that video topic?

Glossary: Metadata. Metadata describes data about data, for certain things such as a video or an image.

Prof. Alga Rhythm

Exactly, Charlie. Let me outline the **KEY CLUES YOUTUBERS** need to give us so that it makes it easier for us to understand what their video is about.

In order for us to understand what your video is about we **read the descriptive words you put in your video upload descriptions.** This gives us **THE NECESSARY CLUES** so that **we can understand what your video is about**. Then we can find groups of viewers / fans that we think would be interested in watching your videos. The video **THUMBNAIL IMAGE** may show to this group of viewers or fans when they search for this video topic.

There are **4 main things** that you can add to your **METADATA** to make your videos appear in front of those fans you think would benefit from or be entertained by watching your videos.

- A **video TITLE** explaining what the video is about. For example: ‘My Top 5 Easy Ways to Make Pizza’.
- A **video DESCRIPTION** of what can be found in the video. What viewers can expect to see. A brief description of your channel. Other relevant video links.
- **TAGS**. These are keywords that describe the video topic(s).
- A **THUMBNAIL image** that represents what the viewer will find when they watch the video.

Prof. Alga Rhythm

Sam, are you going to talk about the details of the metadata later in the chapter?

Sam

I sure am, Alga. Leave it with me. I know you're super busy with **millions of videos to scan**.

Let's be serious – it's unlikely that the whole world would be interested in watching your video on **'How To Train Your New Pet Puppy To Roll Over'**, **RIGHT?** You may want that video to be seen by only those peeps who have a new pet puppy and want to get it to roll over and do other cool tricks (as you can see I'm more of a **DOG PERSON**). Well, **that's my job.** Not to roll over and do doggy tricks, of course, but to **suggest this video to viewers who would be interested in seeing doggy tricks and puppy training videos**.

In some cases, you may want the **whole world to see your video** showing your cat doing its two-legged dance routine before receiving their teatime snack treats! **#CatsOfYouTube**. **Everyone loves a cute cat video**.

These kinds of videos **appeal to A LOT of folks**. Peeps love to **share** the fun and then the video develops a mind of its own and goes crazy. You may know these as **VIRAL VIDEOS**.

Glossary: Viral videos. These videos get lots of views very quickly, usually due to lots of people sharing them in a short space of time.

Q&A

Charlie

How do I make a **VIRAL VIDEO**? (AKA one of the mysteries of the universe IMO).

Prof. Alga Rhythm

Good question but it's not one that has a simple answer, I'm afraid. It **depends on many factors** but one to note is that viral videos tend to keep people entertained so that they watch the full video. The video can be compelling for any reason – funny, informative, action packed or remarkable – it doesn't really matter. What matters is that **viewers keep sharing it with friends and family and then it grows just like a real virus.** I'm pretty certain you have expert knowledge of how a virus spreads **IRL**!

Charlie

YIKES. The less said about that the better!

Prof. Alga Rhythm

A viral video basically follows the same principle of any virus. It's based on the **quick sharing** and **spreading** of something from one person to another making it **contagious**. That's why videos that are shared rapidly are called **VIRAL VIDEOS**.

Many VIRAL VIDEOS tend to be funny videos as people love to share funny things and that's possibly why they go viral. One thing to remember is that **you don't need a viral video to be an awesome YouTube creator**. Early on, most creators don't have a viral video and they **build up their channel gradually and consistently.** Eventually every active YouTube channel has a viral video and it is usually the video with the most views.

Personally, I believe that the **most important thing is to GET STARTED**. If you're doing things the **right way**, your videos will be watched by the right peeps and fans. Whether your videos entertain, teach or inform you can **make a POSITIVE IMPACT on the world with your awesome video skills and creativity.**

RANDOM FACT ALERT

Greta Thunberg was just 15 years old when she raised awareness of CLIMATE CHANGE among kids and adults all around the world. She was so passionate that the way we treat our planet should change for the better she started a global movement to help make a positive change for the environment.

Things are always changing and you never know when changes occur. For example, it's quite possible that **views and subscribers** may be removed one day from public view. That means your viewers won't be able to see these numbers, and only you will see them in your **CREATOR STUDIO** account data.

Views and subscriber numbers are sometimes referred to as **vanity stats**, which just means that they are **surface numbers** and don't hold any deeper meaning.

This shouldn't make much difference to you when you're starting out. It's for this reason it's a **good idea to focus on your brilliant video making TALENTS and not rely on these VANITY STATS**.

To get a deeper understanding of how your channel is performing you need to **look at the 'analytics'** section of your **YouTube studio**.

For example, views and subscriber counts don't exist on cable TV or Netflix (and never have), and they have some of the best films and video series ever. They use **CHARTS** to indicate which programmes are popular. This just proves that it is possible to create amazing films and videos and still have lots of fans who keep coming back to watch more.

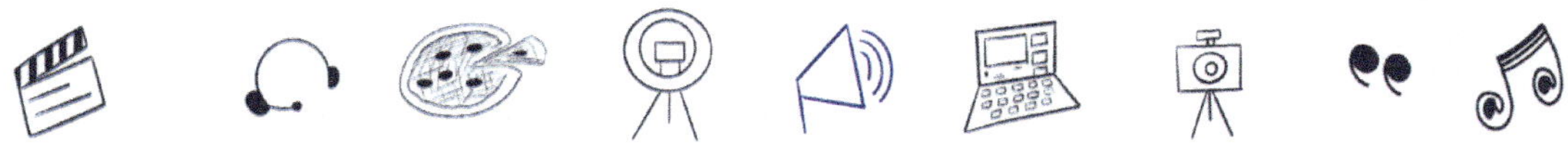

As long as you and your **FFFs** like them, that's all that matters. If you focus on just making great videos that **peeps want to watch** then **views and subscriber numbers don't matter**. Your videos will always be awesome.

TIPS AND TRICKS:

If you're very keen to get a VIRAL YOUTUBE VIDEO then here's a quick HACK.

The trick to getting a video that is viewed and shared a lot is to:

- make a video about 5-10 minutes long
- include anything that might be trending or cover a very popular topic
- make an awesome video about it and upload it while the topic is still trending

I would only recommend doing this if you really enjoy the video topic. It doesn't always work but a lot of viral videos have this in common.

If you want to check how well your videos are doing, check out your 'retention graphs' in the 'analytics' section of your YouTube studio.

These graphs show you how much of your video is being watched. If your graph shows only a few people stay to watch more than one quarter of your video, then perhaps there is room for improvement. If there is a good amount of your video being watched, *for example*, over half, then perhaps you can make more of those types of videos as that clearly shows they are being enjoyed by your viewing fans.

Chapter 7

YOUTUBE PRO

CHAPTER 7: YOUTUBE PRO

HOW YOUTUBE PROS GET MORE VIEWS AND SUBSCRIBERS

Well done on making it to the last chapter of **How to Start a YouTube Channel – The Easy Way**. It's important to remember that creating a YouTube channel is not just about making fantastic videos that you **LOVE CREATING**, but it's also about **serving your community** of friends, family and fans who **love watching your videos**.

However, at the start it can be very tricky to become known as no one has heard of you, and there are literally **BILLIONS** of videos on YouTube.

So how can your potential fans find your **GEM OF A VIDEO** in the video ocean we know and love at YouTube?

As explained in Chapter 6, making sure your video is found is like **leaving a trail of clues** so Professor Alga Rhythm and the team can help find viewers who are interested in your video topic. To find fans, Prof. Alga Rhythm uses something called **search rankings** and **suggested videos** on YouTube. That means your **video thumbnails get shown** to more relevant peeps. In addition, when peeps do a search for something on YouTube, your video may also be **suggested or recommended** to those viewers.

The professor is a little like a detective (think Sherlock Holmes meets AI).

HOW TO BE AN AWESOME YOUTUBE PRO

Let's recap on what we learned from Prof. Algor Rhythm.

BTW, you may hear the phrase 'optimise your video / channel' to describe the clues, but don't let techy words put you off. **'Optimise' is the term given to the act of leaving a really good set of clues** in your video upload description and **metadata**. This is so the computer programme – **the algorithm** – can understand what your video is about and who might be interested in watching it. I think you get the gist of this by now, and I'm sure you don't want me to drone on (not to be confused with **UFCs – UNIDENTIFIED FLYING CAMERAS**) about it anymore, **BUT** I do want to help you understand how to do it.

To do this **properly**, you need to leave clues about your video in the **CREATOR STUDIO** (**sometimes referred to as the BACK END**). As you know, it's so that Prof. Alga Rhythm and the team can figure out who might be interested in seeing the video. **Get your parent(s) or guardian(s) involved at this point as you will need to go into your YouTube account**. You will need help and guidance on doing this the right way, especially as you start out.

Let's go through each main video 'clue' and show you how to **optimise** your video properly so your video can be found by interested viewers.

Video titles

Your video should have an **eye catching and descriptive title**. It needs to grab the attention of the people you want to see it. Think of a great **title that represents what's in your video**. Make sure you use the **keyword(s)** or the main words of your video in your title. This helps the Prof. understand what your video is about. Keywords are exactly that – **a word that is KEY to your video**. It forms part of the **metadata** we talked about in Chapter 6. Or it can be a word that easily describes what your video content is about. For example, a key word for a pizza making video might be 'pizza' or 'pizza making' or 'making mini pizzas'. (You can have more than one word in a keyword, which are sometimes referred to as **long-tail**

keywords.) **REMEMBER** – there is no room for **CLICKBAIT**. You cannot cheat the system. Stick to a title that is relevant to your video.

Glossary: Clickbait is a video, title or thumbnail that looks interesting enough to click onto but it does not truly represent the content of that video.

Video description

The description box is a great place to add extra info and links that you may have mentioned in your video, or offer further information about your topic. **The more information you give here about your video the better chance of the right people finding it**. You can write an essay in the description section, so **GO TO TOWN** if you really want to. You have up to a **WHOPPING** 5000 characters to write about your video. It's a **FABULOUS OPPORTUNITY** to add some of your other related video links too. Take advantage of this space.

I'm not sure who would actually write an essay here but this is a brilliant place to get your viewers to learn more about **YOU, your video** and **your channel**. Writing as much as possible and including some relevant **keywords**, or **'clue words'** as I like to call them, gives you a higher chance of your video popping up and being suggested when people are searching for something on your topic. For example, if viewers are looking for a video on your topic by searching in Google or doing a YouTube **SEARCH**, then your video has a good chance of being suggested to watch.

Video tags

This is a different section to the description area.

YouTube **TAGS** are used for the same purpose as **hashtags**. Tags and hashtags are **keywords** or **relevant words**. Video tags are **specific words** that you use to describe the video. Choose words that reflect what your video is about and what you think people are searching for. There is a **limit of around 500 characters** so be sure to choose the most relevant words that relate to your video. I recommend using between **5 and 15 tags** in this section. For example, if your video is about making a chocolate milkshake then you need to add tags like 'chocolate' and 'milkshake'. Just like your video titles, video tags don't have to be just one word tags. You can use a few words together. For example, you could put 'How to make a chocolate milkshake', 'chocolate milkshake' and 'How to make milkshake' in your tags section.

TIPS AND TRICKS:

- Put your video tags in order of the most popular or most relevant words. This helps you stay focussed and organised!
- You can create your title, description and tags even before you make your video.
- You can add these in your video planner to help you stay organised.
- When filming your videos take some photos of your video content so that you can use the photo images to create great quality thumbnails for your final video upload.

Ted

How do peeps find what they're searching for with all that information everywhere on the internet? It's **MIND BLOWING**.

Sam

It's easy. All they have to do is type a few words about the information they are looking for into the **Google** or **YouTube search box**. I think you can even do a **voice search** too.

Prof. Alga Rhythm

That's right, Sam. **Voice activated queries or searches** are available and use **voice recognition** to suggest relevant answers to search commands. It's exactly the same way that Google Home, Alexa and Siri work.

You heard from him earlier when we talked about **MUSIC** and **VIDEO UPLOADS**, and now I'm going to introduce the amazing **Sammy AKA Sam the Kid** once again. He's the best and **absolutely brilliant** at making the **creator studio** back end work like a well-oiled **MACHINEEROONY.** Here's our creator studio dude.

Q&A

Charlie

Sam, what should we know about creating a **THUMBNAIL** for a **YouTube video**, and what is a **thumbnail** anyway?

Sam

Thanks, Charlie. A video thumbnail is critical for **optimising** the high suggestibility in the **infrastructure** YouTube systems. The **algorithm uses AI** to infer the connections between the graphic format and the derived video content clues and **configurations**.

Charlie

WHOA WHOA WHOA...hang on a minute!

Have you swallowed the entire official YouTube handbook? Perhaps we can try another way of explaining.

Let's try a **KISS** approach.

Sam

I beg your pardon!?

Charlie

KISS – Keep It Simple, Sweetie.

Sam

Oh, I see, why didn't you say? Let's do this...**SIMPLE** all the way from now on, I promise.

Video thumbnails

Your video thumbnail is the image you see on **YouTube** videos. It's the image or photo that represents your video. It's like having a **visual title**. If you don't add your own '**custom thumbnail**', or don't have one ready when uploading your video, YouTube gives you a choice of **3 selected frames from your video**. You can select one of the frames that **best represents what's in your video**.

The algorithm can actually read the image. It can understand what's on the image (as well as what's in the video) using **machine learning mechanisms**.

Charlie

Hey Bro, go easy on the technical jargon. Remember **KISS**?

Sam

Oh yeh, sorry about that. What I basically mean is that **each video has a thumbnail**. This is an image that you can create in any graphics app such as Canva or Photoshop. I'll give you some more suggestions in the Backstage area in Chapter 8.

Sam

When you have an image (thumbnail) ready, you can upload it to your video in your YouTube's channel creator studio.

How to make a super cool thumbnail

Your thumbnail needs to **stand out** otherwise the peeps might not click on it. You want it to look fun and appealing so that the intended viewers will **click**, **watch** and **enjoy** your video.

First of all, **create an image** that represents what's in the video so that it **attracts attention from your potential fans and viewers**. For example, if you have made a video about how to make a headband for your pet (which is a great idea BTW, unless your pet is a fish!) then you create a nice **clear, close up image** of the finished headband on your pet and put this image as the video thumbnail.

You can also **add a bit of text on the image**. **Don't use too many words** and make sure the text is **relevant** and **big enough** to read on a small device like a smart phone.

Use **contrasting colours**. Use **bright colours** on the image and **cool text fonts** so they stand out and get noticed.

Charlie

What's the **'rule of thumb'** on how to create a thumbnail? (I couldn't help myself. ;))

Sam

Nice one, Charlie!

To create a **GOOD THUMBNAIL** you will need a **graphics app**. As mentioned, I use Canva, PicsArt, PicMonkey, Procreate and Adobe Spark. I've been using Canva for a long time and I find it the easiest to use. I know lots of YouTubers who use many different graphics apps but Canva is the easiest **IMO**, probably because I've been using it **forever**!

For example, if you use Canva, follow these steps:

- Download the app onto your computer
- Insert your chosen thumbnail image or photo into Canva
- Select a 'new design' with the right image size for a YouTube thumbnail, which is 1920 x 1080 pixels (Canva has ready-made YouTube thumbnail templates)
- Select the text font, colour and size
- Add any filters
- Export as a **.JPEG** or **.PNG** file
- Add to your creator studio video upload
- **You're DONE!**

Personally, I love making thumbnails; it really brings out the **creative** in me! You can **use any image for your video thumbnail** – it can be text, a photo or a drawing – just so long as it shows what the video is about. For the best results use the **YouTube thumbnail image size of 1920 x 1080 pixels** which allows for a design based on the **golden ratio** (basically, it's a landscape rectangle). It's a great shape to work with and makes **outstanding looking thumbnail creations**. Good luck and have **FUN**!

RANDOM FACT ALERT

Did you know that the GOLDEN RATIO goes back centuries and is a mathematical ratio also written as 16:9? This shape is found in nature and known to be the most aesthetically appealing to the HUMAN EYE, so it works perfectly in design. The golden ratio has been used in CINEMA, and FILMAKERS still use it today.

Charlie

I LOVE movies! Check out **Charlie Chaplin's** classic movie video **'The Kid'** – my favourite video ever! (BTW, we might share the same first name but we're not related.) It was made 100 years ago and it's still going strong. Now that's what I call entertainment.

Vertical (AKA portrait) filming will never **cut it**. These video shorts and vertical videos might be challenging the old **horizontal (landscape)** filming habits on which the golden ratio is based, but will it last?

Sam

Speaking as a video making traditionalist, it's certainly a challenge, Charlie. But you could never really watch a long video or movie in vertical or portrait mode, could you? **It just doesn't feel comfortable**. There must be something in that **golden ratio** thing.

Ted

I could watch it for a short while, I guess.

'Cut it' nice pun Charlie. BTW, what happened to your hair? Looks cool!

Prof. Alga Rhythm

I don't get it. What's a pun anyway? And BTW, I agree with Ted, I like the new esthetic.

There are a few other important factors to consider when you're trying to grow your **YouTube** channel and want to get your videos seen by new potential fans.

Video watch time

Watch time is a big help when it comes to your videos being discovered in the YouTube universe.

Marvela

What the heck is **WITCH TIME?** Something to do with Sam's **optimisation wizardry** or perhaps the spell of the golden ratio?

Sam

It's not as exciting as that I'm afraid, Marvela. I like your style though, very imaginative! **I rather fancy an optimisation spell, how about** **OPTIMVIDIARMUS?.**

Anyway it's not **'witch time'**, it's **'WATCH TIME** and alas there are no **spells involved**!

Marvela

OPTIM-VID-IAR-MUS. Cool – I like that.

Sam

Basically, it's another important **CLUE** that tells Professor Alga Rhythm and the **watch team** that you have a wonderful video that people would love to watch. **Watch time is a measurement of the length of time that people watch your video**.

Here's something for you to think about. **Do your fans watch your video until the end?** If so, the prof. will think it's great and recommend it to even more potential viewers and fans.

Or, **do peeps only watch the first few seconds of your video?** If so, then the prof. won't think it will be interesting to many other peeps, and alas won't show it to many new people.

So, if you want more people to see your videos, and want to grow a **COMMUNITY** then your job is to **make sure your videos are interesting and entertaining** enough to keep your viewers watching until the end.

Basically, the longer someone watches your video the more valuable it becomes, and the more likely Professor Algor Rhythm is to encourage new viewers and fans to watch it.

Charlie

BTW, you might not be at this stage yet if you're just starting out. It sounds quite advanced but I guess it's good to know. Great video can be defined as **video that people actually want to watch**. Am I right, or am I right?

Sam

You're quite right. Thank you for that. Shall I go on? Is my explanation simple enough?

Charlie

It's perfect. Carry on, don't let me interrupt.

Charlie

Ooops, sorry, just another QQ. What about our **YouTube community** – how do we go about building our community, or tribes or fans or viewers or whatever they're called?

Sam

Thanks for reminding me, Charlie. It's an excellent question although I wouldn't call it a quick question. Let me explain...

Let's talk about **building a COMMUNITY**. This is something that comes after you have **mastered the art of video making**.

It might even be something you want to concentrate on when you're a bit older or when you've had lots of video making practice. If you're 16/17 or under I would suggest, like I did previously, talking through your community and channel growth with your parent(s) or guardian(s). They can help you and keep watch on all the **privacy settings** that you need to put into place.

See the backstage area (Chapter 8) for details on online safety and privacy, for kids and parents / guardians.

That said, let's continue...

HOW TO BUILD YOUR COMMUNITY

Sometimes known as tribes, fans or followers, these are people who want to be part of your **COMMUNITY.** Your community are made up of the peeps who are interested in seeing your videos, and that's why they watch and subscribe to your channel. They don't want to miss your latest awesome video and **they want to be part of what you create**. They feel like they have something in common with the other peeps who watch your videos.

The more you create and upload awesome videos that your fans like to watch, the more likely you are to find people who want to **subscribe to your channel**. To **grow your YouTube community,** you need to make sure you're creating videos that:

1. People are looking for, enjoy and appreciate.
2. Are uploaded consistently – perhaps one every 2 months if you're just starting.
3. Remind your viewers to subscribe to your channel.
4. Leave those **clues** in the form of relevant and great video titles, descriptions and tags.
5. Contain a fabulous thumbnail image.

Charlie

Optimise to the max! or should I say **OPTIM-VID-IAR-MUS**?

Sam

And that's pretty much it. Oh, and remember to always remind your **community** of the **rules**, such as being **kind**, **thoughtful** and **respectful** when making comments within your community and in all social media communications.

With all that said and done, you will start to gain lots of viewers and subscribers. These **special peeps are the ones who look forward to watching your every new video** as soon as it's released.

They are also likely to **share** your videos with friends and family. They may also start to comment in the comments section below the video. The **comments section is a great place where fans of your video and YouTube channels can discuss various subjects with you – the YouTube creator – and each other.**

REMEMBER: In order to keep things **safe for kids** a lot of YouTube promotional features are turned off. For example, the community tab, iCards and end cards, as well as comments, are all turned off for kids' channels for **safeguarding reasons**. This is good as you don't want to get distracted with unwanted comments, and it allows you to focus on making awesome videos.

Charlie

Good point. When we attract more attention to our videos and grow a community or tribe, **we YouTubers need to lay down the law – OUR LAW for the COMMON GOOD!** It's not the **WILD WEST** anymore. It doesn't matter what your channel is about, if it's a gaming or beauty or whatever channel, your community needs to enjoy being part of it. To **keep a happy atmosphere in the community**, YouTube creator pros need to set out their boundaries.

In other words we have to **remind the community how to behave and stick to the channel rules**. I advise my fans that any unsavoury remarks or behaviour will not be tolerated. If I see any **TROLLING** or **HATE** in my community then I **EXPEL THEM FOREVER**! It sounds **DRASTIC** but it's gotta be done. (I can **BLOCK** their account and report them to YouTube.)

See the backstage area (Chapter 8) for information on online safety, CYBERBULLYING and SAFEGUARDING.

Video comments

Ask your viewers to get involved and comment in the comments area. COPPA rules mean that kids' channels and channels targeting kids don't have this feature anymore. But it's something you can explore as you and your community get older and continue on your YouTube journey.

Glossary: COPPA is a USA body and stands for Children's Online Privacy Protection Rule. It imposes certain requirements on website owners that target children aged under 13.

Once you're 16/17 and have your own YouTube channel, and still want to be a pro YouTuber creator, you can focus on your community comments and interactions more frequently. In the meantime, ask your parent(s) or guardian(s) to get involved so they can manage this side of things **so you can get on with the fun part of making awesome videos**.

Q&A

Ted

What do I do about trolls and haters? I'm never sure what to do when I see a comment or video that makes me feel bad.

Sam

First of all, if you have a channel for kids, you shouldn't be seeing any comments so get a parent or guardian to **check your YouTube account settings**. If you do see any messages or comments on other channels that look negative or mean, you should always tell a parent, guardian or teacher immediately. Whether it's your channel or someone else's you should report these comments by clicking the three dots on the top left hand corner of each comment, then click **REPORT**.

If it's your account you can **ban and block the troll and ZAP them into OBLIVION** and keep them out of your space and community.

Marvela

Find out more about **staying safe online** in the Backstage section (Chapter 8). There's lots of help out there for you. This is not a battle you can fight alone so it's better to **ALWAYS REPORT** anything that makes you feel uncomfortable, however little. Always **SPEAK UP** and **SPEAK OUT**. It's important.

Charlie

It's difficult to know exactly **why haters do what they do.** They're more than likely just having a bad hair day, bored, or just plain naughty, or are trying to make you feel bad because they feel bad. There could be many reasons **BUT it's IMPORTANT to know that you don't have to accept being part of their 'bad day'.**

Ted

What's a bad hair day?

Charlie

Never mind about the hair.

Haters want to get **your ATTENTION** so it's better not give it to them as it will encourage them to do it more.

Better to **ZAP than TAP !!!!!!!!**

The main thing to remember is that if they disrupt the pleasant atmosphere and **GOOD VIBES** of your channel, or they say mean or rude things, then they **don't deserve to be part of the community.** Therefore, they should be blocked from your channel and **banished from your channel kingdom for good.**

Prof. Alga Rhythm

Please also ask a parent or guardian to help check your settings and disable comments if they are not already disabled. If you feel bad or upset about anything you see or read on the internet, or on YouTube, speak to an adult immediately.

See the backstage area (Chapter 8) for online safety links and CYBERBULLYING and SAFEGUARDING support.

Cherrybelle

My question is about creating images. What graphics and image making tools should I use to make thumbnails, story boards, channel artwork and other related digital pictures?

Sam

There are so many. I know Charlie uses Canva. I use PicsArt and Procreate as I can use them on my tablet and smartphone. Photoshop, After Effects and Gimp are more **advanced graphics software**, which I personally find easier to use on my desktop / laptop computer. You can do a lot of advanced stuff with these but **the apps I mentioned earlier are quick and easy to use**.

See the backstage area (Chapter 8) for recommended graphics apps, graphic design software, free to use images and video footage sites.

THE FUTURE OF VIDEO MAKING

Looks like that's a wrap everyone. There are so many other exciting subjects to talk about when it comes to YouTube, such as how to **make money** from your videos, how to **collaborate** with other YouTubers, how to **live stream**, and how to make your videos look like **cinematic productions**....but let's get your channel off the ground before we talk about any of that stuff. You've got plenty of creative video making practise to get on with until then, and lots to look forward to learning.

It's so exciting that you have come this far and **thank you** for letting me and my friends guide you on the start of your pro YouTuber journey!

Once you have spent some time creating your videos, uploading them to your channel and becoming **YouTube awesome**, remember to **give me a MENTION.** Maybe we could even do a collab one day?!

And lastly...

Always remember to do your best. Your videos don't have to be purrfect. You will always be learning new things about video but the principles remain the same: **focus on your video topic ideas and talents, plan your production, filming and storytelling**, and **upload consistently** or whenever possible. **REMEMBER** that you don't have to overdo it and you can keep your videos on **PRIVATE** for as long as you want. You can keep your videos for your own personal memories. You should release them and make them public only **WHEN YOU ARE READY** and you have **ASKED PERMISSION** from your parent(s) / guardian(s). The most important thing is to enjoy what you do, have fun and do it for yourself and your **FFFs** as I'm sure they will be cheering you on all the way, as I will be.

Charlie

I hope we have given you some ideas about making YouTube videos and helped you understand how to **do it the easy way.** Good luck and, most of all, enjoy your video making journey!

Marvela

Enjoy making videos, and **stay organised!**

Ted

Remember, editing takes time so pace yourself and enjoy the process. **Remember KISS** when you start out.

Cherrybelle

Let your imagination take centre stage, **embrace the drama and GO FOR IT.** Love making videos.

Sam

Same as Ted. Let me leave you with a KISS: Keep It Simple, Sweetie. Enjoy your **unlimited creative powers with video.**

Prof. Alga Rhythm

I'll be looking out for your videos. Go forth, **unleash your talents** and make your ideas come alive with video!

CIAO FOR NOW AND GOODBYE...

A few last words from me. First of all, **congratulations** on reaching the end of the book. From my personal **YouTube** creator experience, I can honestly say that **making video is my favourite thing to do,** in case you missed that.

If you don't have the **VIDEO MAKING BUG** yet you soon will have (just so long as it's not any other kind of bug, ahem, mentioning no names!). **REMEMBER** that **YouTube** is about **a steady PACE, it's not a RACE**. It's like the story of the Hare and the Tortoise (a classic tale – check it out). There's no hurry. **It takes time and practise** to become a pro. If you really want to be a video creator pro, keep experimenting, see what type of video you enjoy making, find out more about yourself and your interests, be authentic, get your family involved and keep making those videos. (It's much easier than writing and illustrating a book like this one.)

YOU ARE THE NEXT YOUTUBE CREATOR GENERATION AND IT'S BEEN A PLEASURE TO HAVE YOUR COMPANY.

Be **responsible**, be **respectful**, be **creative** and, most of all, **enjoy making video.**

THANK YOU FOR READING

WE WISH YOU GREAT VIDEO MAKING FUN AND SATISFACTION.

BYE -ADIOS – CIAO- AU REVOIR – NAMASTE – ADJO
CHARLIE and FRIENDS

HAVE A GO: DO FUN TASKS & CHALLENGES IN CHAPTER 8.

See the backstage area (Chapter 8) to pick up your Video Making Enthusiast & Proficiency certificate and lots more.

Chapter 8

BACKSTAGE

YOUTUBERS BEYOND THIS POINT ONLY

CHAPTER 8: BACKSTAGE CONTENTS

Resources: Some clickable pages and the online safety section in this chapter can be downloaded at my website OnlineMediaBiz.com/Books

WELCOME FROM AROUND THE WORLD

Your challenge: Can you name which countries these languages are from and can you say them out loud?

ようこそ -

Hola -

Receber -

Bienvenue -

καλως ΗΡΘΑΤΕ -

Välkommen -

Herzlich willkommen -

Namaste -

Sveik -

Welina -

Velkominn -

Bienvenidos -

Bine ati venit -

Benvenuto -

Selamat datang -

欢迎 -

Witamy -

Mirëseardhje -

어서 오십시오 -

Добродошли -

स्वागत है -

Chào mừng -

Croeso -

Selamat datang -

Welkom -

Maligayang pagdating -

خوش آمدی

Hoşgeldiniz -

Mirëseardhje -

Gratissimum -

Uyemukelwa -

Vítejte -

Dobrodošli -

أهلا بك-

Добре дошли -

Soo dhawow -

ברוך הבא -

ยินดีต้อนรับ -

Добро пожаловать -

Velkommen -

Translations according to Google translate - thank you. Answers on next page

MESSAGES FROM THE PROS

With a combined total of over 10 million subscribers and 3 billion views, these inspiring YouTubers have some very special messages and advice for you!

THE WALL OF YOUTUBER WISDOM

Maggy Woodley
YouTube.com/RedTedArt
@redtedart

One thing to bear in mind, is to always stay safe online! That means not giving away the location of your house or your school. It is so easy to "accidentally" film a logo on a school blazer or mention a very local shop. This has happened to me a number of times. But don't fear - simply do a "jump cut" in your editing or overlay an emoji and edit that kind of information out of 99% your viewers won't even notice a small part is missing!
Maggy

Connor Colquhoun
YouTube.com/CDawgVA
@cdawgva

Don't aim to become a YouTuber, aim to become an entertainer who can captivate an audience on any stage.
Connor

Oli Greaves
YouTube.com/ogxtailor
@ogreavesx

The great thing about YouTube is that you can tell your story however you like. However, when you are editing your video, think about how you can keep your audience's attention. The first 10 seconds are key, so make sure it is exciting and a taster of what is coming up.
Oli

Dan Bull
YouTube.com/DanBull
@insdanbull

Make content about things you love and have always loved. Chasing trending topics can get you some quick exposure but if that's all you do, you will not end up with videos that people will keep watching for years to come. It's also far more enjoyable to immerse yourself in a project you really care about. Your audience will tell how much fun you're having, and fun is contagious. Also, try and get enough sleep.
Dan

Don't give up if you do not succeed at first. Success takes a long time. All YouTubers started small. Just have fun! People will see, if you are having fun or not. You should be proud of what you are doing. People look up to someone who is brave, confident and like what they do. And don't be afraid of haters. They are just jealous that you are brave enough do something they don't.
Sunshine

Sunshine
YouTube.com/SurpriseCollector

Don't forget - always do a quick recording test to check that your recording setup works before recording your videos. It's really annoying when you finish your gameplay and commentary and then find your video wasn't recording.
Sam

Sam
YouTube.com/SamTheKidGaming

MORE MESSAGES FROM THE PROS

Lucy Wyndham-Read
YouTube.com/LWRFitnessChannel
@lucywyndhamread

My advice is go with your heart and be true to yourself. Don't be scared to be different when it comes to publishing your content. YouTube is an incredible platform to share your passion and skill with the world. And with anything in life if you work hard and believe in yourself you can turn your Channel into a great success because this platform is here for everyone.

Lucy

Emma Drew
YouTube.com/MyVoxSongs
YouTube.com/NurseryRhymes
@myvoxsongs

If you don't want to be on camera yourself, explore different video styles like animation, stop motion, motion graphics, silhouettes, time lapse, art & crafts with an overhead camera or try screen capture for gaming videos. Explore the art of video making and find out which types of video you enjoy creating.

Emma

Luke Ayios
YouTube.com/MiffedCrew

Don't look at views and subscribers too much. Be in it to enjoy it, attention will come as you grow with it. Make use of the community tab as it goes to the algorithm and subscribers like it. Make use of all the free training that's out there. Familiarise yourself with those in your target community, join in with them, know what works for them. Start with what you can, gain experience. Quality beats quantity which you will improve as you develop.

Luke

In the early days of YouTube everything was new and untried. These days there are channels for everything and standing out in the crowd is tough. Doing what's popular once could get you places but now just risks you getting lost in a sea of other channels all competing to grab the trends. The best advice I can give is to look for the sort of content you want to see but can't find, then make it yourself! Be that a whole new thing or just your own unique twist on an established formula. Because if you want to watch it you can be sure there are other people out there looking for it too and that's a whole audience waiting to find you!

Greg

Greg
YouTube.com/TheStupendium
@thestupendium

Aaron Abke
YouTube.com/AaronAbke
@aaronabke

It's really important to stay inspired when you're creating content for YouTube. That means you can't spend all your time and energy on YouTube or you will eventually "crash and burn". The last thing you want is to create content because you "have to". Do things that inspire you. Watch movies, enjoy nature, go on a trip, find a hobby you enjoy. If you're excited about your content, your audience will be excited to watch it! That's how you grow a channel and build a loyal audience that loves watching your videos.

Aaron

THE WALL OF YOUTUBER WISDOM

Why You Want To Be A YouTuber. The Quiz.

I want to become a YouTuber because I want to...
(tick all the reasons that apply to you)

- [ ] have fun
- [ ] be a full-time YouTuber pro when I'm older
- [ ] have fans and followers
- [ ] teach people what I know / can do

- [ ] share my gaming videos
- [ ] be an influencer

- [ ] share my music
- [ ] entertain people with my talent, comedy, music, art
- [ ] create pranks or challenges
- [ ] share my opinion and review stuff

- [ ] sell merch
- [ ] help change the world to be a better place
- [ ] give me something to do and be less bored
- [ ] be rich
- [ ] become the biggest YouTuber ever
- [ ] make YouTube & Netflix series originals and movies
- [ ] be a cool filmmaker
- [ ] talk about history
- [ ] talk about my POV

- [ ] learn how media works
- [ ] be famous
- [ ] other (write your reasons below)

____

____

____

YOUTUBE CHANNEL DESCRIPTION EXAMPLES & FUN TASK

Why, what and who examples.

Further examples of YouTube Channel descriptions

Example 3:

I want to start a YouTube channel about hair for people who enjoy hairstyles and creativity because I want to inspire people to learn and enjoy creating cool hairstyles so that they can have a go at home.

Example 4:

I want to start a YouTube channel for budding dancers about my life as a dancer because I want to share my tips, choreography and experience with my videos that show my daily routines, variety of my dance video shorts and warm up tips.

HAVE A GO:

Write your own YouTube channel description

Fill in the blanks below to describe WHAT kind of channel you want to start, WHY you want to start it and WHO will enjoy it.

I want to start a YouTube channel about

(add your main topic /category)

☆

for(add who you expect will watch your videos)

☆

because I want to (add why)

☆

with my videos that show(your video content ideas).

☆

VIDEO MAKING PLANNER

USE THIS PAGE AS A REMINDER ON HOW TO PREPARE AND ORGANISE A VIDEO. CHECK OFF EACH OF THE FOLLOWING AS YOU PREPARE.

1. Create video idea & storyboard

2. Write script

3. List equipment needed

4. List of props or costumes needed

5. Find filming space

6. List graphics & video editing apps / software

Plan your video

The A-Z of equipment and items you may need

Use this checklist to help identify what you need for your video. You won't need everything listed below. Just tick those things you think you need.

- [ ] Camera / recording device (tablet, phone, webcam, screen capture)
- [ ] Camera holder: Tripod / selfie stick / something to hold camera or rest it against
- [ ] Editing app or software
- [ ] Green screen / green fabric or background wall
- [ ] Headphones
- [ ] Helpers, pets, friends & family
- [ ] Laptop / PC / device
- [ ] Lighting / daylight / lamp(s) / ring light / window light
- [ ] Microphone
- [ ] On / Off Air sign
- [ ] Pen and paper (anything to write notes and ideas)
- [ ] Props / toys / objects / subjects / models
- [ ] Screen capture app / software
- [ ] Studio area / filming space
- [ ] Script
- [ ] Storyboard

YOUTUBE CHANNEL HOMEPAGE DESIGN

HAVE A GO: SKETCH OUT HOW YOU WANT YOUR YOUTUBE CHANNEL TO LOOK. ADD SOME TITLES AND DESIGN YOUR BANNER ARTWORK AND THUMBNAILS IN THE BOXES BELOW

YOUTUBE CHANNEL BANNER ARTWORK

YOUTUBE CHANNEL NAME & ICON IMAGE

CHANNEL VIDEO DESCRIPTION

VIDEO TRAILER

HOME | VIDEOS | PLAYLISTS | COMMUNITY | CHANNELS | ABOUT

UPLOADS

VIDEO TITLE:

VIDEO TITLE:

VIDEO TITLE:

VIDEO TITLE:

PLAYLIST TITLE:

VIDEO TITLE:

VIDEO TITLE:

VIDEO TITLE:

VIDEO TITLE:

DESIGN YOUR YOUTUBE CHANNEL THUMBNAIL EXAMPLES - SKETCH IDEAS

YOUR VIDEO STORYBOARD

SKETCH & DESCRIBE.

The simple way to start planning your video

	beginning	middle	end
Step 1	Sketch out what you would like to see at the beginning of your video.	Sketch out what you would like to see in the middle of your video.	Sketch out what you would like to see at the end of your video.
Step 2	Describe what you want to say, do or show in the first part of your video.	Describe what you want to say, do or show in the middle part of your video.	Describe what you want to say, do or show at the end part of your video.

Step 3

YOUR VIDEO STORYBOARD

SCRIPT YOUR SCENES.

The easy way to start planning your video

intro script

beginning script / scenes

How many scenes do you want in the beginning of your video? 1, 2 ,3 or more? Can you write a description and script for each scene?

Scene 1

Scene 2

Scene 3

middle script / scenes

How many scenes do you want in the middle of your video? 1, 2 ,3 or more? Can you write a description and script for each scene?

Scene 1

Scene 2

Scene 3

end script / scenes

How many scenes do you want at the end of your video? 1, 2 ,3 or more? Can you write a description and script for each scene?

Scene 1

Scene 2

Scene 3

outro script

USEFUL APPS & SOFTWARE

Remember to ask for permission and supervision from your parents/guardians before downloading apps or subscribing to software.

Graphics, images & video sites

IMAGES:
Pixabay
Pexels
Unsplash
Canva

Animation apps & Software

APPS:
FlipaClip
Stop Motion Studio
Stop Animator
Vimage

SOFTWARE:
Toon boom
Stop Motion Studio-
ClipStudio Paint

Recording apps

LIVE ACTION FILMING APPS:
ProMovie
FiLMiC Pro

SCREEN CAPTURE (DESKTOP):
Stream labs / OBS
Screenflow
Quicktime Player
Windows screen recorder

Audio sites, apps & music software

SITES:
YouTube audio library
Epicdemic sound
Stock.Adobe
Premium Beat
Audio jungle

APPS: Acapella,
Voice record Pro

SOFTWARE:
Garageband
Audacity
Logic (goodnfor music)

Graphics & image apps

APPS:
Canva
PicMonkey
Procreate
PicsArt

SOFTWARE:
Gimp
Photoshop
Affinity
Photoshop Express
Paint.NET (Windows)
Adobe Express

YouTube learning sites, apps & tools

YouTube Studio app
YouTube Kids app
YouTube.com/creators

Management & research tools:
Tubebuddy
VidIQ
Social Blade

Editing apps

APPS:
CapCut
InShot
Canva
YouTube Create
Davinci resolve
PerfectVideo Movie Maker
CuteCut
YouCam Cut
KineMaster-
VideoEditor&Maker
iMovie (Apple)
Clips (for iPhone)
CutStory
Video Editor

SOFTWARE:
Final Cut Pro
Premiere Pro Rush
Davinci Resolve
Microsoft Photos (Windows
Movie Maker)
Lightworks
Filmora

*Download this page at OnlineMediaBiz.com/Books for clickable links

USEFUL VIDEO & RECORDING EQUIPMENT

HERE'S SOME EQUIPMENT, APPS & SOFTWARE THAT MAY WANT TO CHECK OUT. (ALWAYS DO YOUR RESEARCH BEFORE BUYING EQUIPMENT & APPS)*

Remember to ask for permission and supervision from your parents/guardians before downloading apps or subscribing to software.

Cameras

Mobiles / Smart phones
Tablets
Compact Digital Camera
DSLR Cameras -
(I've used : Canon 250D
Nikon 5300)

Webcams

Webcam with Microphone

Webcam light

Lighting

Camera lighting:

Ring Light with Tripod

LED lighting kit

Fairy Lights

LED Strip Lights

Chairs

Ergonomic Gaming Chair

Microphones

Snowball
Blue yeti
Rode
Lavier for smartphone

Headphones

Turtle Beach Gaming Headset with mic

Mpow Gaming Headset

Green screen

Green Screen fabric

Green Screen kit

Gaming green for chair

Collapsible Green screen blind

Accessories:

Multi-Color LED Keyboard & mouse combo

Hand held / selfie adjustable mini tripod

Tripod with overhead & sife angles

*Download this page at OnlineMediaBiz.com/Books for clickable links

VIDEO INTRO / OUTRO SCRIPT

Example scripts to stick up in front of you while filming

Intro script

Hi, welcome to my channel about
....(fill in)
In this video I'm going to show you
....(fill in)
So, let's get started!

Outro script #1

Thanks for watching. Please subscribe if you want to see more videos like this. See you next time.

Or Outro script #2

If you'd like to see more videos about
....(fill in)
then check out my other videos
about...(fill in)

HAVE A GO:

Write your own YouTube video intro and outro script

INTRO SCRIPT:

OUTRO SCRIPT:

ON AIR
Quiet please:
RECORDING IN PROGRESS

TED
ALGA
CHARLIE

MARVELA
SAM
CHERRY BELLE

OFF AIR
Thank you for your patience:
RECORDING
HAS FINISHED

SILHOUETTE CHARACTERS

Cut around these silhouettes and stick a straw, twig or lollipop stick to one side. Then use them in shadow puppet videos. Make your own shapes or use models or toys to get GREAT SHAPES.

ANIMATION FLIPBOOK CHALLENGE

HAVE A GO: Cut out all 12 boxes/frames. Hold your pile of images in the right number order to make a flipbook. Hold with one hand and flip the book with the other hand to discover what moves are being made. The individual images combine to become one moving image. Can you see what exercise moves I am doing? Try copying the exact 12 frames into your animation app, press the playback button and see your images come alive with video. Experiment with different moves.

ANIMATE-A-SEQUENCE CHALLENGE

HAVE A GO: Create your own animation and flipbook

Draw on your own stick arms and legs (and ears) in different positions on the images below. Each frame should look slightly different. Then cut out all 20 boxes / frames. Hold your pile of images together with one hand (in the right number order) and flip the book with the other hand. You should now see your drawings become one moving image. Try to copy or import your images into an animation app, playback your animation and see your images come alive. Congratulations on your animation!

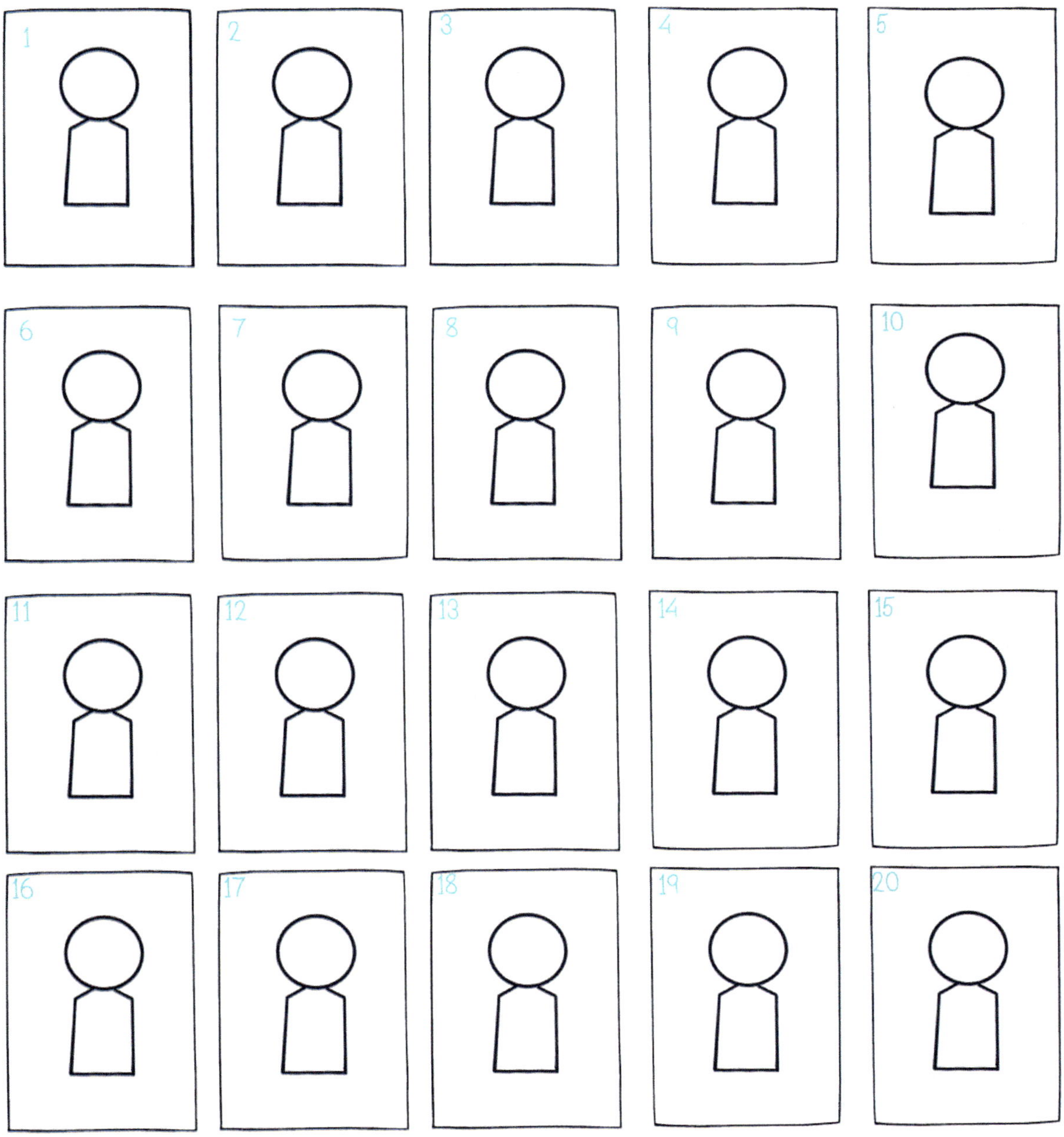

ANIMATION: HAVE A GO:
Create your own animation flipbook sequence

1	2	3	4
5	6	7	8
9	10	11	12
13	14	15	16

COMPOSITION VIEWFINDER

HAVE A GO: Cut out the middle rectangle to create a viewfinder hole. Use this view finder to help you find a good composition for your videos.

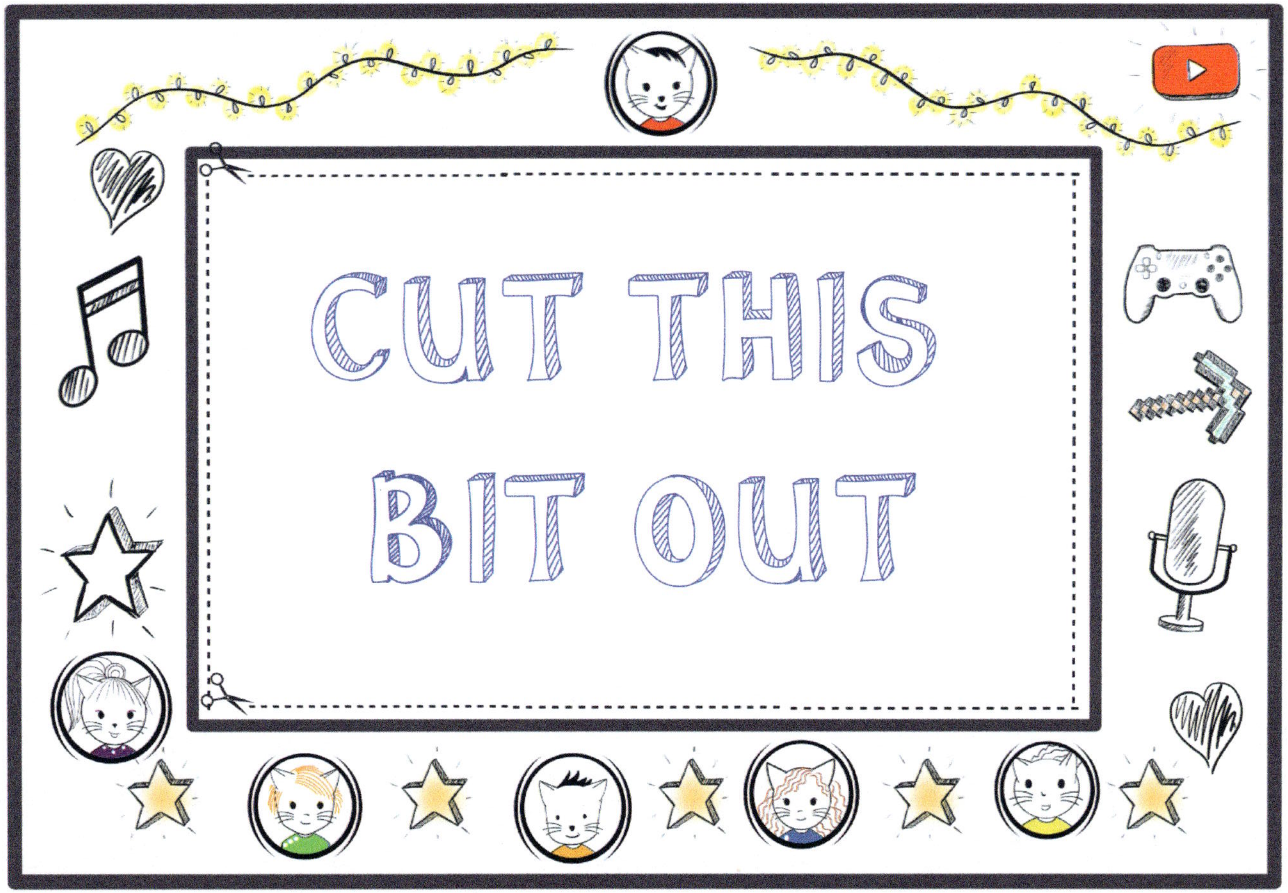

YOUTUBE HELP, LEARNING & SUPPORT

YouTube Channel Help

Minimum age requirements: https://support.google.com/accounts/answer/1350409

YouTube community guidelines: https://www.youtube.com/howyoutubeworks/policies/community-guidelines/#community-guidelines

Account security and tips for staying safe online:
https://support.google.com/youtube/answer/2802848?hl=en&ref_topic=9386941

Get a custome URL: https://support.google.com/youtube/answer/2657968?hl=en-GB

Is your content 'Made for Kids' check: https://support.google.com/youtube/answer/9528076

Copyright: https://www.youtube.com/intl/ALL_uk/howyoutubeworks/policies/copyright/

YouTube creator education: https://www.youtube.com/creators

Staying safe on YouTube

Staying safe on YouTube: https://support.google.com/youtube/answer/9563682?hl=en&ref_topic=9386941

Staying safe as a teen: https://support.google.com/youtube/answer/2802244?hl=en&ref_topic=9386941

Best Practices for Content with Children: https://support.google.com/youtube/answer/9229229?hl=en&ref_topic=9282435

Parents & Families Resources

YouTube families & parent resources: https://support.google.com/youtube/answer/2802272?hl=en

YouTube parent resources: https://safety.google/families

Parental controls and settings: https://support.google.com/youtubekids/answer/6172308?hl=en-GB

Child safety on YouTube: https://support.google.com/youtube/answer/2801999?hl=en

Parent resources: https://support.google.com/youtube/answer/2802272?hl=en

From the book: How To Start A YouTube Channel-The Easy Way With Charlie & Friends

GLOSSARY (A-Z)

Algorithm. According to YouTube, their **algorithm** is a coding system (or computer programme) that is able to show viewers videos that are relevant to their interests, topics and hobbies. It likes to find the right video for the right viewer at the right time.

Artificial intelligence (AI) refers to machines that are programmed to think and behave like humans by copying human actions. The term can be applied to machines that appear to act like the human mind in the way they learn and problem solve. Artificial intelligence (AI) is the refers to machines that are programmed to think and behave like humans by copying human actions. The term can be applied to machines that appear like the human mind, such as learning and problem-solving. It refers to all sorts of data points including voice activation and image recognition.

Authentic. Adjective. Of undisputed origin and not a copy; genuine.

Clickbait is a video, title or thumbnail that looks interesting enough to click onto but it does not truly represent the content of that video.

COPPA is a USA body and stands for Children's Online Privacy Protection Rule. It imposes certain requirements on website owners that target children aged under 13.

Copyright. When someone creates a piece of work they own the work and it is protected by **copyright**. This means no one else can use it without permission.

Copyright strike is when Person A uses music written, created and owned by Person B. Person B protects their work with a copyright and can ask YouTube to remove Person A's video if they haven't asked and received permission to use it. YouTube then removes Person A's video to comply with copyright law.

Custom URL. If eligible, you can give fans an easy-to-remember web address, called a custom URL, for your YouTube channel. This will look like: youtube.com/yourcustomname or youtube.com/c/yourcustomname.

Editing apps allow you to 'glue' all your photos and film footage together to create your final video.

Frame-by-frame animation changes the image in every frame so that when the different frames are put together as one they appear to be moving.

Green screen. This refers to the coloured background or object you want to make transparent before replacing it with another image or alternative video footage for the final version of the video.

Keying. This term is used to describe the green screen removal process in video editing apps and software.

Metadata. Metadata describes data about data, for certain things such as a video or an image.

Monetise is the term YouTube uses for its official program that allows users to make money from the clips they upload. Monetisation most often applies to YouTube creator pros that become a YouTube *partner. To become a YouTube partner and monetise your YouTube channel videos you need to have at least 4000 minutes watch time and have had 1000 subscribers in the last 12 months.*

Post-production *editing is the process of putting your video together and all the extra work done once it has been filmed and recorded, like adding all the video clips together, adding special effects, transitions, filters and music.*

Publish*. A YouTube video can be uploaded but is only seen by viewers when it is made live or published. YouTube has three settings for each video: published, private and unlisted.*

Ring lights and soft boxes *are a form of lighting equipment that help video and film makers create effective and desired lighting effects as well as light up a dimply lit set so that a better quality image can be captured.*

Royalty free *is unowned music and sound that is available for anyone to use for free.*

Video content *is basically all forms of video you see on the internet. This includes vlogs and animations as well as live and recorded videos. YouTube creators often refer to their videos as their* ***video content****.*

Video style*. The ways in which videos are produced and ideas are conveyed to the viewing audience.*

Viral videos. *These videos get lots of views very quickly, usually due to lots of people sharing them in a short space of time.*

YouTube channel homepage*. This is the main YouTube channel webpage. It contains the channel menu, channel artwork, description about videos, a trailer video and all uploaded videos. YouTube creators can customise their homepage.*

YouTube's community guidelines *are designed to protect the YouTube community. They outline what is and isn't allowed on YouTube. This includes video content, comments, links and thumbnails.*

YouTube Play Buttons *form part of the YouTube Creator Awards. They are a series of gifts from YouTube that aim to recognise those channels that have climbed to the top of the charts. Each channel is reviewed to make sure that it follows the YouTube community guidelines before an award is given out.*

WELCOME FROM AROUND THE WORLD

Challenge answers

ようこそ - Japanese

Hola - Spanish

Receber - Portuguese

Bienvenue - French

καλως ΗΡΘΑΤΕ - Greek

Välkommen - Swedish

Herzlich willkommen - German

Namaste - Hindi

Welina - Hawaiian

Sveik - Lithuanian

Velkominn - Icelandic

Bienvenidos - Spanish

Bine ati venit - Romanian

Benvenuto - Italian

Selamat datang - Indonesian

欢迎 - chinese

Witamy - Polish

Mirëseardhje - Albanian

어서 오십시오 - Korean

Добродошли - Serbian

स्वागत है - Hindi

Chào mừng - Vietnamese

Croeso - Welsh

Welkom - Afrikaans & Dutch

Selamat datang - Malay

Maligayang pagdating - Filipino

خوش آمدی Persian

Hoşgeldiniz - Turkish

Mirëseardhje - Albania

Gratissimum - Latin

Uyemukelwa - Zulu

Vítejte - Czech

Dobrodošli - Slovenian & Bosnian & Croatian

أهلا بك-Arabic

Добре дошли - Bulgaria

Soo dhawow - Somali

ยินดีต้อนรับ - Thai

ברוך הבא -Hebrew

Добро пожаловать - Russian

Velkommen - Norwegian & Danish

Translations according to Google translate - thank you.

ULTIMATE VIDEO MAKING AWARD

This is presented to

____

A FANS-TASTIC YOUTUBE CREATOR

CONGRATULATIONS

HELP & SUPPORT FOR KIDS
While making and sharing videos online is fun...
staying safe online is VERY IMPORTANT!
What do I do about haters, rude comments or things I see and read online that upset me?
Great question! One way to STOP THE SPREAD of haters and inappropriate rudeness is to do the following.
Tell a parent, family member or teacher immediately.
Together you can...
1. REPORT
and
2. DELETE
and
3. BLOCK
...any unwanted content
Sometimes when I'm on social media I get a bit stressed when I see bad words said to people I like and follow. What should I do?
Wait. I see that too! Thought it was just me. We need to tell a parent, right?
Yeh but if I tell my parents, they'll think it's my fault and they won't let me go online anymore.
While there's lots of fantastic stuff on the internet, very occasionally you may find something that upsets you or make you feel uneasy. First of all you don't need to feel bad about it, it's not your fault. But it is important to tell someone.
We can't stop having fun because of a few peeps behaving badly. Our job is to highlight the bad stuff and try to stamp it out.
Your parents/guardians and teachers want to keep you safe and will thank you for sharing. They know what to do. They can also check out the internet support groups listed at the back of this book for lots more help and guidance.
If you feel uncomfortable about anything you see online or generally feel unhappy or sad but dont feel able to speak to anyone close to you - you can talk to these supportive groups. They are trained to help kids. Check out the links below and get in touch.
Yeh! A PROBLEM SHARED IS A PROBLEM SOLVED!
What if I keep getting unwanted messages or DMs from random peeps? It's annoying but I don't want to be rude and ignore them.
LOVE THAT!

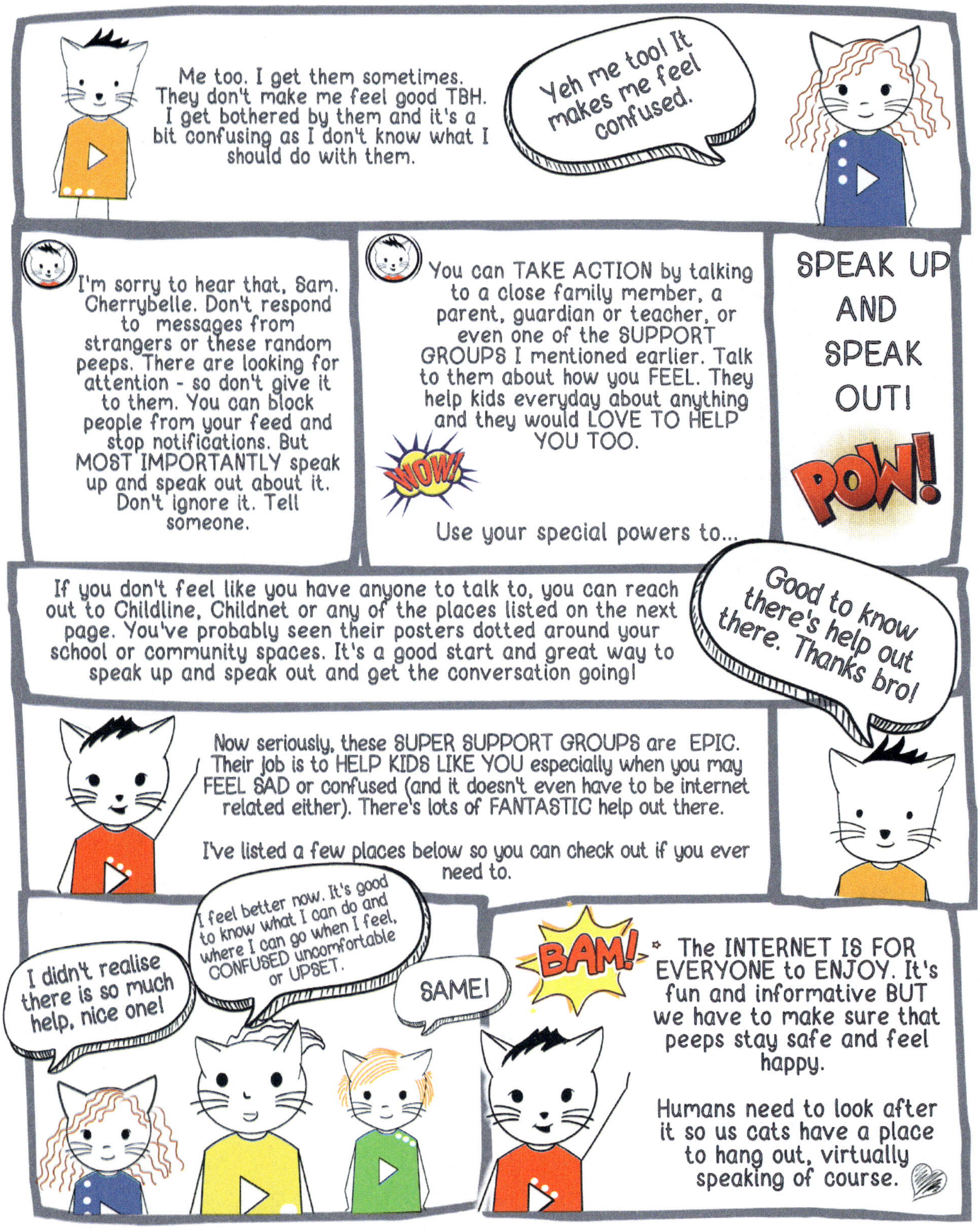

CYBERBULLYING IS NOT O.K.

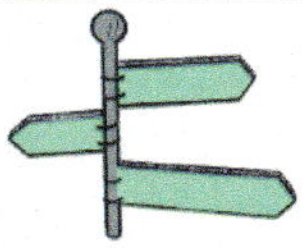

STAY SAFE ONLINE
HELP & SUPPORT FOR KIDS

CYBERBULLYING IS NOT O.K.

YOUR FEELINGS MATTER

If you experience cyberbullying, or bullying of any kind, whether it's haters, upsetting messages or content, talk to your parents, guardians or teachers about how you feel.

If you don't know who to talk to then reach out to the support groups for kids. These special support groups offer an easy way to connect and a safe space to chat online about anything that upsets you. They are there to help you feel better so get in touch with them.

If you FEEL uncomfortable with anything you see or hear on the INTERNET, however small you think it is, please tell a parent, family member, guardian or teacher. You can also contact one of the friendly HELP sites listed below who CARE ABOUT YOU and want to know that you are SAFE and HAPPY.

STAY SAFE ONLINE
SPEAK UP AND SPEAK OUT

From the book: How To Start A YouTube Channel-The Easy Way With Charlie & Friends

Check out these helplines, textlines and online chat services for kids.

Childline

Childline.org.uk

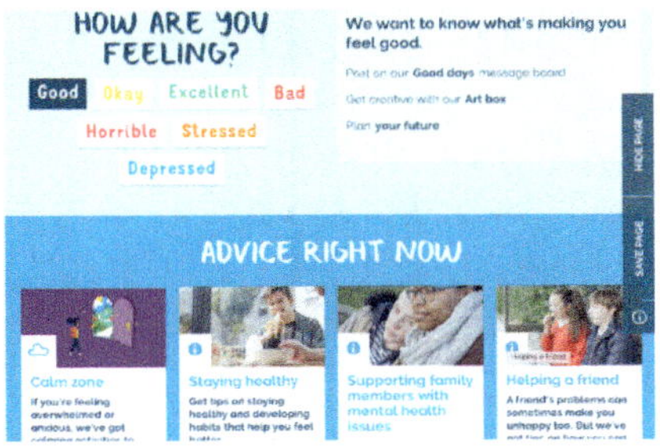

Kooth

kooth.com

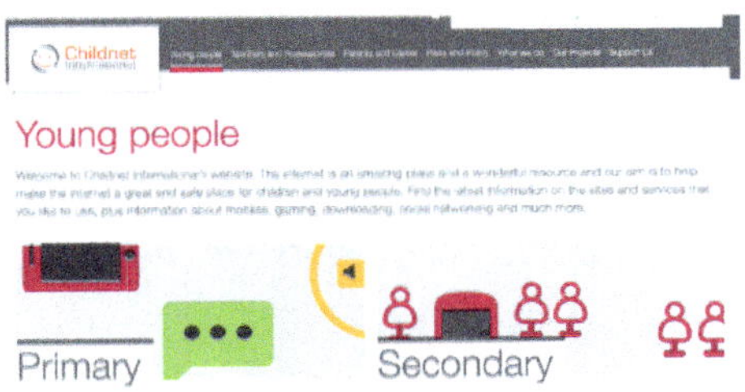

Childnet International

childnet.com

Samaritans

samaritans.org

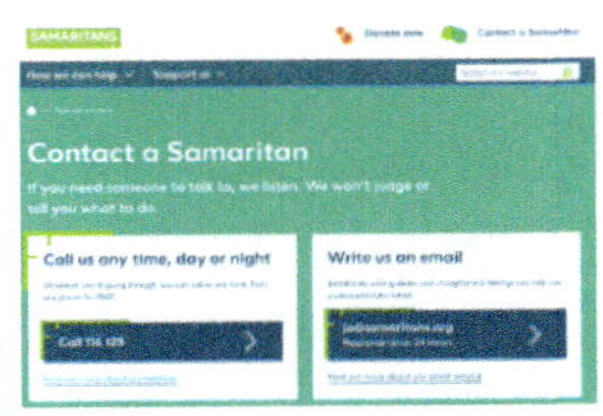

Giveusashout.org (UK)

Crisistextline.org (USA)

ABOUT THE AUTHOR

Hi there,
I'm Emma the creator of this book and when I was young I loved drawing. Lucky for me then, my last name is Drew. I have a YouTube channel called MyVoxSongs where I create original animations set against popular nursery rhymes and songs. I've also got cool URLs: YouTube.com/NurseryRhymes and YouTube.com/MyVoxSongs.

I've been making videos before YouTube even existed, so it's no surprise that I became a YouTube creator. Not only did I become a video creator, but my kids also created their own videos when they were just 8 years old.

We are a video family through and through. My kids love spending their spare time creating videos for fun. In particular they like making stop motion, green screen, skits, Minecraft and react videos. They even edit their own videos. I always encourage them to find ways to make interesting videos, whether it's by using animation tools and special effects, or by finding interesting props.

Before becoming a YouTuber, I worked for Simon Cowell on Pop Idol and The X Factor. I saw so many talented young people but only a few got the chance to show their talent, and even fewer actually won the shows. With YouTube, everyone is a winner as everyone has the opportunity to share a talent and entertain family, friends and fans.

Nowadays, I spend my time helping new creators start their YouTube channels with my tips and advice. Last year I talked to a large audience about how to start a YouTube channel at VidCon IRL. Lots of people and kids were very keen to get started. I also had fun interviewing YouTubers Blanks, Wilbur Soot, Lee Hinchcliffe and AdamB about their YouTube channels. I even did a short skit backstage with wacky and wonderful YouTuber Hacker The Dog (yes, he's a real dog!). The VidCon community rocks!

I believe that video is an amazing way to share your talents, knowledge, opinions, music and ideas. People make videos for many reasons - to share privately with family and friends, to keep as memories, or to entertain hundreds, thousands and millions of people around the world. Whatever you want to do with your video making skills, just remember, video is a fantastic way to share something special with special people.

I hope that this book 'How To Start A YouTube Channel - The Easy Way!' helps you think about ways to you can make your special videos too. Have fun, stay safe and most importantly enjoy yourself. Emma

ONLINE SAFETY RESOURCES
for
PARENTS, GUARDIANS & TEACHERS

From the book: How To Start A YouTube Channel-The Easy Way With Charlie & Friends

A note from the author

I have been navigating the evolution of our virtual world over the years while also conscious of my kids internet needs for creativity, school, leisure and development. Personally, I have put simple things in place to help manage internet use at home. These include regular conversations with my kids on what they are watching online. Taking a particular interest in the details of their favourite influencers and content.

It's fair to say that like me, most parents face a constant challenge to monitor and manage their kid's online usage and it's often difficult to know where to start looking for help and information. With this in mind I have outlined some great starting points for further information on the subject of online safety for kids and support for children's mental well being.

These organisations have an enormous amount of expertise and offer a great deal of useful information, guides and support for both parents, teens and kids and people of any age. The internet is part of our children's daily lives and will be an integral part of their future. I hope this information supports and encourages you to learn more about the help that is available to make the global internet community become a safer place to enjoy and learn.

Learn more about where to get support, how to protect your kids online and make a difference

NSPCC

https://www.nspcc.org.uk/keeping-children-safe/

Childnet International

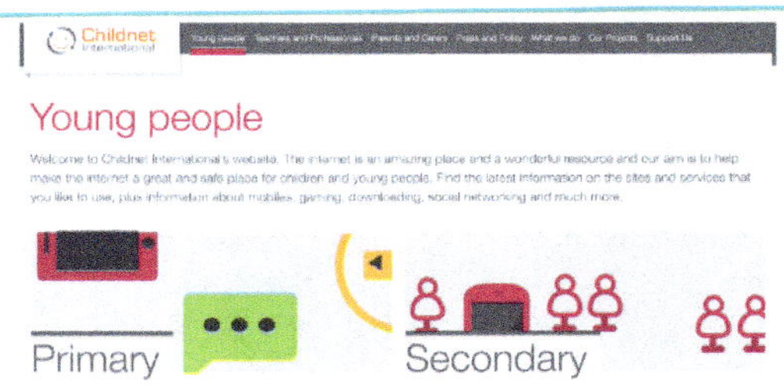

https://www.childnet.com/what-we-do
https://www.childnet.com/resources/supporting-lgbt-children-online

Internet Matters

https://www.internetmatters.org/

The Diana Award

https://diana-award.org.uk/anti-bullying/

ONLINE SAFETY RESOURCES for PARENTS, GUARDIANS & TEACHERS

Young Minds ParentsGuides

https://youngminds.org.uk/find-help/for-parents/parents-guide-to-support-a-z/

YoungMinds

https://youngminds.org.uk/

Place2Be

https://www.place2be.org.uk

UK Safer Internet Centre

https://www.saferinternet.org.uk/

NHS Every Mind Matters

Self-care and social media

Lots of us clock up some serious hours online, so let Jade Laurice and her friend KB share tips on how to avoid getting stressed from socials and what else they do to feel good.

Dealing with change

Sometimes we feel fine and in control when things change, but at other times we get worked up and stressed out. Super Sam and Helen share tips, tech and advice to help you chill and de-stress.

Dealing with unhelpful thoughts

We can all have negative thoughts sometimes. Learn how to step outside yourself and stay on top of your feelings – and do not hesitate to get further support if you're really struggling.

The Worry Tree

Learn about a great way to stop you from dwelling on things you cannot control and refocus your mind on the choices you can make. And remember: it's always OK to ask for help if you need it.

hhttps://www.nhs.uk/oneyou/every-mind-matters/youth-mental-health/

Think U Know

What information are you looking for?

Professionals
working with children and young people

Parent or carer
help children get the most out of the internet

4 - 7
years old

8 - 10
years old

11 - 18
years old

https://www.ceopeducation.co.uk/

ONLINE SAFETY RESOURCES for ADULTS, PARENTS, GUARDIANS & TEACHERS

Further information regarding online safety, digital parenting, laws and relevant articles

Common Sense Media

https://www.commonsensemedia.org

Center For Humane Tech

https://www.humanetech.com/

Online safety law - articles & sites - US, UK, Australia

The Internet Police

Child Exploitation and Online Protection command

A National Crime Agency command

www.ceop.police.uk/safety-centre

https://www.childsafe.org.au/help-for-families/e-safety-online/

https://www.childsafe.org.au/help-for-families/e-safety-online/

You can download these handy online safety resources at: https://onlinemediabiz.com/books/ (Please note: These resources are just a few helpful suggestions based on my research into online safety and are not an exhaustive list – keep searching, help is out there!).

Printed in Great Britain
by Amazon

52431849R00126